PREVENTING BRANDSLAUGHTER
How to Preserve, Support,
and Grow Your Brand Asset Value

David M. Corbin

Introduction by Hyrum W. Smith,
President, Franklin Covey

D0557486

ISBN-13: 978-1514725993

Dedication

With love, respect and admiration I dedicate this book to the many caring, courteous service providers who have left a positive impression in my mind and heart. You are the embodiment of brand integrity. For some, this is quite natural behavior. For others, this level of service quality and brand integration comes from serious dedication to learning how to fully live the brand. Either way...You rock!

Acknowledgements

In the process of writing this book, I've been blessed with quite a few gifts in terms of insight, counsel and more. Of note, Patti McKenna has been brilliant in her role of editor, writer, creative guru. I also thank Rekhaa Gopinath, my 'go to' for so many activities and projects and who has contributed to Preventing BrandSlaughter with her creation and execution of the book covers, pagination and much more. To my many mentors through my career, many living and some passed, I endeavor to honor you with my effort and hope that this book extends your contribution even further. Finally, I acknowledge the brilliant and gifted thought leader and business icon, Hyrum W. Smith, for his kind confirmation of and belief that this book is going to add massive value in the field of brand integrity, I say Thank You Sir for that and for your wonderful Introduction of the book.

What People Are Saying ...

"David Corbin's model of Preventing BrandSlaughter was foremost in our culture of building and preserving the Pictionary brand. Read this book now."

-Rob Angel, Founder/Inventor Pictionary

"David Corbin's books and speeches are loaded with brilliant, instantly useable ideas on how to deliver extraordinary service to everyone, every time."

-Mark Victor Hansen,   co-creator #1 New York Times best-selling series Chicken Soup for the Soul

"We all know that having a brand is critical. What Preventing BrandSlaughter teaches is even more critical because it shows everyone how to 'live' the brand all the time. All of our service and business associations would do well to adopt this philosophy now!"

-Frank Shankwitz, creator and co- founder Make-A-Wish Foundation

"This story and the lessons contained are essential for anyone or any company who wants to be a Champion in their field. I learned on the long path to the Olympics that integrity is the true breakfast of champions. And Preventing BrandSlaughter teaches how to maintain and support brand integrity with every employee, every day. I give this book a gold medal."

-Ruben Gonzalez, Four time Olympian in Luge, bestselling Author, award-winning Speaker

"I love reading a good story as much as working on one. Preventing BrandSlaughter is a wonderful story in which we learn that we're either supporting our brand with our behaviors or we're destroying it. And what I love most about it is that it gives us a specific strategy to keep ourselves and our teammates on track to living the brand in integrity and avoid committing BrandSlaughter. Now THAT fosters a true brandcentric culture."

-John Christensen Creator of The Fish! Philosophy and Co-author of the international best-selling book Fish

"Your ability to deliver excellent customer service will determine your success or failure. David Corbin will show you how."

-Brian Tracy, author, Eat That Frog

"We know it's all about goals and a major goal of your business is to create and grow your brand. In this book you will learn specific ways to do just that...and not fall prey to *BrandSlaughter. In my company we do the brand audit regularly to protect and preserve our brand and reputation."*

-Gary Ryan Blair, best-selling author, Everything Counts.

"It was a great pleasure working directly with David Corbin. His no nonsense methods that are clearly spelled out in Preventing BrandSlaughter and his dynamic workshops and consultations helped revitalize our brand. Together, working with front line and executive stakeholders we developed a culture to keep up with the shifting market place and the demands of our customers".

-David J. Gilman Consultant at Kaiser Permanente Vision Essentials and Small Business Owner.

"David Corbin is the Master at teaching you how to create your brand, how to sustain your brand and how to make money from your brand. So remember, you need to prevent BrandSlaughter and you start by reading this book."

-Sharon Lechter, co-author Rich Dad Poor Dad and Outwitting The Devil

"My mentor, David Corbin, has developed ideas, strategies and systems that will help you achieve enormous success and prosperity....and peace of mind. They certainly work for me!"

-Greg S. Reid, co-author, Think and Grow Rich: Three Feet from Gold

"This quick read will boost your business value immensely. Implement these lessons and as a business broker I can get you top dollar for your business when the time is right."

-Michelle Seiler Tucker, President Seiler Tucker, Inc.

"Over the past 15 years I have invited David to present both to industry experts in healthcare as well as world class medical device manufacturers. A key point he made in many of those discussions was to illuminate the negative to get to the positives. This radically changed the "customer care" approach with both patients and healthcare professionals resulting in significant increases in sales and quality measurements."

-Ron Richard, CEO, Nitetronic LL and President/CEO of BLD Consulting LLC

"The essence of a brand is simple: it's a promise. Its execution is another matter. David Corbin brilliantly articulates the importance of keeping that promise in every aspect of your business: from within, outward. His allegorical approach is accessible and brings his teaching to life. Preventing Brand Slaughter is for every business person bored by experts. It's a book for the rest of us."

-Ross Halleck, Founder/CEO Halleck Vineyards, CEO Brand Strategist, Halleck Inc.

"As a health care designer I have witnessed the importance of Brand Integrity in all forms of communication, the physical environment and the culture of the organization. David's teachings and parable in Brand Slaughter is a great tool for organizations to both guide and reinforce health care leadership's journey to customer excellence."

-Annette Ridenour, CEO, Aesthetics, Inc.

"In the almost 30 years I know David Corbin he continues to astound with his unique insights, prescient prophecies and unconventional wisdom. He established a new service standard showing us how to be Psyched on Service. In Illuminate... Harnessing the Positive Power of Negative Thinking, he blasted a meteor-sized hole through conventional "positive thinking." Now, with Preventing BrandSlaughter he adds another masterwork to his brilliant collection. You won't just read this book. You'll highlight it, mark it up, take notes, dog-ear the pages and come back to it over and over again to remind you how vital it is to maintain brand integrity. Whether you're a global business or a brand of one, this book is essential for every leader who cares about Preventing BrandSlaughter."

-Mitch Axelrod, #1 best-selling Author, creator of The NEW Game of Business™ and The NEW Game of Selling™

"David Corbin's PREVENTING BRANDSLAUGHTER is the most important book for the "C" suite in 30 years. The investment in "brand" voice is the essence of success in a world where IP is the value and the brand is the voice of the IP value. To risk brand slaughter is to unwind everything. The safe base for any leader seeking to protect their brand space is to read BRAND SLAUGHETER with a market pen making TO DO lists in the margins as I did. CEO SPACE ranked # 1 Biz Conf in the world by Forbes and Inc....I can't afford to slaughter the brand ...can you?"

-Berny Dohrmann, Chairman CEO SPACE International, Author Film Producer, Radio Host, Top Ranked Forbes Keynote

"David Corbin has a way of stating things that gives one a simple perspective and immediately usable tools to not only grow but to polish your business and your brand. This book is a gem because it gives you specifics on how to do just that. There is nothing more valuable than an instantly recognizable brand that is well loved. As a business owner with multiple franchises, I continue to value David's insight and knowledge."

-Michael Szawielenko, Owner Operator of over 30 IHOP Restaurants President/CEO Hotcakes Inc dba IHOP

"Not only does Dave produce measurable results he also is a pleasure to work with. Dave has developed innovative techniques to stimulate our employees, being able to create highly motivated staff. Dave delivers concise well-organized presentation creating an extreme amount of enthusiasm to all."

-Ralph Steinberg, Director of Operations, Kaiser Permanente Vision Services

Table of Contents

Introduction

In this book, Preventing BrandSlaughter, David Corbin outlines, in the form of a parable – the story of Reliant Hospital – how essential brand is to the foundational responsibility of any organization – attracting, engaging and keeping top performers.

The brand, as a tangible expression of a top performing culture, comes to life when its elements – including the mission – are taken off the wall and put into daily action at all levels and through all individuals in the organization. This occurs, and is measured through, what David calls "ABI" – the Audit of Brand Integrity – are we living our brand?

That ABI process surfaces whether your brand is growing or dying or standing still (which means, dying). As in the example of "Bubbas Ribs", the health of the brand is a function of how well his team were delivering on that brand to their customers. A failure to deliver the brand results in BrandSlaughter- the quick and painful or slow and unrelenting death of the heart and soul of the organization – its brand.

Every day, with your brand in the hands of each and every employee, permeating each and every interaction with customers "one bad apple CAN spoil the whole bunch."

Returning to the Reliant Hospital story, David points out how integrity to the internal and external brand whether you're a world-class surgeon or a security guard at the front entrance to the building matters. If anyone, at any time, decides something "brand essential" is not their job that internal failure will translate into external brandslaughter.

David builds on the idea of internal and external brand integrity with a metric he calls "the 4 C's – cleanliness, communication, caring and compassion" and then tracks their seemingly mundane yet powerful effect in the day to day operation of the hospital.

As his model builds, David points out how to be both proactive and productively responsive in building a brand, growing it and, above all else, Preventing BrandSlaughter. A commitment to excellence and a "no room for error" mentality forms the backbone of the proactive expression of brand while clearly defined, brand focused, and preventative measures shore up the necessary responsiveness in a constantly changing environment.

Creating, in the whole team, but most especially in leaders, a commitment to staying informed, seeking out new and better ideas and testing those ideas in the crucible of a successful brand are essential to continued success and brand expansion.

Finally, a commitment to regular brand audits as ways to identify strengths and weaknesses and build proactive responses to both shows how the cultural and interpersonal elements of a business need the same types of attention, tools and focus as the technical elements usually receive. This holistic approach to organizational leadership stresses that all three elements – brand, people and technical- come to bear on organizational outcomes and brand success vs. slaughter.

For years I've taught and our own company has emphasized the very principles David outlines in this book. What makes his work special and very much worth your time is his ability to clarify the concept and to quantify the steps you must take to take brand concepts off the wall and put them to work in the day to day operations of your organization and, in doing so, to guarantee you'll never face the terrible specter of "BrandSlaughter".

-Hyrum W. Smith, President, Franklin Covey

Prologue

Throughout the years, I've worked closely with companies and organizations to assist them in many aspects, including improving employee morale, building support and uncovering issues that threaten to tilt the balanced environment they've created. I've also been privileged to speak to audiences and business groups, providing them with techniques and strategies which effectively maximize their productivity and profitability. Whether I'm relating the benefits of top-notch service or leading a business through the challenges wrought by change, I've found that every business and organization owns one common thread that, if broken or weakened, can threaten even the most successful organization—their Brand.

A brand is much more than a logo, an image stamped on pencils and stationary, embedded in a website, or displayed on a sign. It's the compilation of all aspects of a company, grouped together to portray a larger picture than a custom logo. Your brand speaks to your clients, customers, and community, telling them about your business philosophies and practices. It is conveyed through every encounter your business has with the public, who become buyers of your brand—not your product or service.

The many facets of your brand are linked together to create your company's image. In the end, your image will be only as good as your weakest link. It's been said that people don't acknowledge excellence often, but they will never fail to point out flaws. I've seen it many times—a business has an outstanding product, but poor customer service, an organization provides excellent care to its customers, but treats its staff and employees with indifference. The smallest of flaws have the power to fleck and mar the image of the business and weaken its brand.

What really is a brand? It's the entire look and personality of a business. It's so important that it's bought and sold, along with a company's physical facilities, inventory, name, and logo. This proves that it has real, measurable value. So, when a brand is weakened or destroyed, there will eventually be a loss of income or revenue to the business. Like a crime, the destruction of a brand is a theft from a company's image and net worth. That's why I call the undermining of a brand "BrandSlaughter."

Don't be the victim of external or internal brand homicide. This book will show you how to protect your brand by revealing the many ways people commit BrandSlaughter. You'll meet Walker Briggs, Chief Security Officer, who sees all and knows all, CEO Phillip Dobbins, and Duncan Edwards, who introduced the BrandSlaughter program to the hospital's staff and is charged with implementing the program and training their employees. Inside Reliance Hospital, you'll see how every employee can positively, or negatively, impact an organization's brand as they go from their day-to-day activities and face their biggest challenges in an institution that is continually striving to meet the needs of the most demanding customer—the community and every member in it.

The intentional or unintentional death of your brand is

preventable, but only if you are aware of the accomplices and acts of BrandSlaughter within your organization and learn the strategies to protect your most important asset—your brand.

Welcome to Reliance Hospital

Standing outside the main entrance of Reliance Hospital, Walker Briggs scanned the grounds, as he had done thousands of times before. His eye caught a piece of paper which had blown into the flower bed to his right, and he quickly picked it up and tossed it in the trash. As Chief Security Guard, Briggs' job description didn't include maintaining the beauty and cleanliness of the hospital, but at Reliance, no one was exempt from doing their part to uphold the hospital's image. If it needs to be done, do it, Walker had often told his staff. After double checking to make sure that nothing else was out of place or no one needed assistance, he was satisfied that everything was in order for today's orientation.

Walker preferred to stand post at the main entrance, especially on Monday mornings. A tall, broad-shouldered man with a smile as big as his stature, he greeted the employees returning to work from their weekend, calling them all by name. He'd spent most of his career at the hospital and knew just about every one of its employees. They knew they could count on Walker, too, and could practically set their watches for his daily walk-through each department. If there is anyone who knew everything that went on within the hospital, you can bet it's Walker.

Today, Walker stands ready to direct new employees and volunteers to the hospital's auditorium, located in the lower level across from the cafeteria. He'd been told to expect a large group, close to 100 or so, and his trained eye was rarely wrong as he identified those approaching the revolving doors as visitors or new employees.

"Welcome to Reliance Hospital," he said to several new faces. "If you need assistance or directions, please stop at the reception desk just inside the doors." After repeating this greeting several times, he noticed a familiar face. It must be 7:45, he thought as he saw Phillip Dobbins crossing the parking lot, briefcase in one hand and cell phone in the other. Like clockwork, Dobbins entered the hospital at the exact same time every day, and Walker was there, rain or shine, to greet him.

Dobbins had been CEO for two years, and during that time, he'd made major changes in the hospital. Today's orientation was the second under his command. All employees are mandated to attend one. Walker had been at Reliance for 20 years, and he, too, had been required to attend one of several sessions Dobbins and Vivian Daly, the Human Resource director, had devised last year to teach them about the

hospital's new mission and brand. The goal was to create an image to every employee, supplier, guest, and patient who walked through the doors that Reliance was an institution which provided excellent healthcare in an efficient, caring environment. No employee was exempt from the mission—no matter what their role or level of hierarchy, it was their responsibility to work together with all other employees to increase the quality of services and the satisfaction of their patients, providers, staff, and visitors.

"Good morning, Mr. Dobbins." Walker's greeting was accompanied by his signature smile.

"Hello, Walker. How's everything going this morning?"

"Just fine, sir. Just fine. A little busy with the new group coming in today, but everything's going smoothly."

"That's good to hear," Dobbins replied. "Let me know if you need anything."

"I'll do that, sir," said Walker, as he stepped aside to let his boss enter. But Walker knew that he probably wouldn't need anything. He knew his job like the back of his hand and was good at it. It was a message he knew the new employees in today's orientation would also receive. It didn't matter if they were surgeons, nurses, technicians, cooks, or security guards like him, they all knew how to do their job. But that's not what the orientation was about. As Dobbins had told every employee and would repeat again today, "You already know your job and the skills you'll need to fulfill your duties. Today, you're going to get to know Reliance Hospital."

First Impressions

Softly closing the door behind him, Phillip Dobbins entered the back of the hospital auditorium, quickly scanning the group below who were being indoctrinated into the Reliance family. It looks like everyone is here, he thought, noting that the auditorium was at near half of its seating capacity. He took a moment to admire the room once again, pleased with its renovation. *Yes, the remodeling we requested had produced the desired effect—one that is elegant in an understated way, functional, yet warm and inviting.* Dobbins knew that impressions were everything, which is why he had stressed the importance of an environment which was inviting and friendly. His purpose had been to create a balance between the cold and functional style of a sanitary medical facility and the warmth of a caring, comfortable institution which welcomed its patients and visitors. The rich tones of the leaf pattern in the carpeted stairs and seating area contrasted nicely with the polished cherry wood floor at the front of the room. The deep gold upholstery of the seats pulled the room together. One hardly noticed the large overheard monitor and technical equipment behind the podium.

"Welcome to the Reliance family." Dobbins' thoughts were interrupted by the introductory words by Vivian Daly. Always punctual, the Human Resource Director was right on cue—opening the orientation at precisely 8 a.m. "Today, you're going to learn about Reliance, our mission, and our values. And, you're going to learn how important your role in carrying them out is to our facility and the community we serve."

PREVENTING BRANDSLAUGHTER

Noting that Vivian was following her orientation script to a tee, Phillip approved. *Start with our mission—everything revolves around it. That mission is our brand—it's the most important part of everything we do,* he thought.

"You might have noticed," continued Vivian as she clicked a wireless mouse and turned to the large monitor behind her, "this mural on the wall in the entrance of Reliance Hospital." Instantly, the screen displayed a photograph of the mural, hand-painted by a local artist who had turned their mission statement into a six foot work of art. "We are proud to openly display our mission to our visitors, patients, and vendors. Throughout the hospital, you'll notice other places where it is displayed for public viewing—it is posted in every elevator, on every department's bulletin board, and in every waiting room in the hospital."

This was something Dobbins had insisted on. It was vital to their hospital's brand that their mission statement receive maximum exposure. In fact, in his opinion, it was the only way he could ensure that they stayed true to the values which had made Reliance one of the top hospitals in the nation.

From that point, Dobbins listened to Vivian as she read the mission statement in its entirety. He closed his eyes and recited the words in his head from memory, knowing that before long, every new employee in the auditorium would be able to do the same.

Life is an extraordinary journey, and the quality of every step is impacted by health.

At Reliance, our mission is to provide healthcare experiences that are just as extraordinary.

We are dedicated to providing remarkable service to each and every person who enters our doors, regardless of their circumstances.

At all times, we strive to provide the highest quality of care, our kindest touch, and our strongest commitment to excellence.

With another click of the mouse, the core values of Reliance flew onto the screen.

- **Integrity**
  We respect human dignity and promote honesty, fairness, and equality.

- **Excellence**
  We are dedicated to providing clinical, operational and service excellence based on the cornerstones of safety, confidentiality, accountability, teamwork, and commitment to high value.

- **Partnership**
  We work in cooperation with care providers and the community, guided by open communication, trust, and shared decision-making.

As Vivian began reading the last of the core values, Dobbins straightened his tie and readied himself for her upcoming introduction.

"Now, I'd like to introduce you to the President and CEO of Reliance Hospital. Phillip Dobbins came to Reliance two years ago after an extensive search to find someone to lead our facility as we continue to grow and embrace our commitment to our largest investment—our employees, patients, and community."

On cue, Dobbins began his trek to the podium, stopping for a brief moment as Vivian returned to the microphone.

"I should point out that Mr. Dobbins is the youngest CEO that Reliance has ever had. But don't let that fool you—he brings with him a vast record of accomplishments in healthcare administration. While he may not yet be gray around the temples, that certainly doesn't mean that he's wet behind the ears," she laughed, using the cliché to lighten the mood. It was also a good way to inject the private joke she and Dobbins shared after she confessed to him that, initially, she had been concerned that he was too young to have the experience and such a high-level position required. Boy, had he proven her wrong.

Laughing, Dobbins approached the podium. "Thank you, Vivian, for what I believe was a positive introduction."

Now able to see their faces, Dobbins scanned the new employees seated across the auditorium. He had already met some of them. Chiefs of departments, physicians, and surgeons were required to receive his stamp of approval before being recommended to the Board of Directors for hire. Among the familiar faces, he quickly identified Drs. Wang and Jacobsen, as well as Alexander Barrett, their new chief cardiac surgeon with a specialty in non-invasive robotic cardiac surgery, a procedure that Dobbins was excited about adding to Reliance's cardiac unit. He also noticed Nanette, a patient account processor, who had worked at Reliance previously and had taken a leave to stay at home with her adopted daughter for a year. A lot can change in a year's time, thought Dobbins, and previous employment didn't exempt any employee from attending the mandatory orientation.

"Vivian has already covered our mission at Reliance Hospital, but I want to take this opportunity to expand on that mission and tell you how it will impact you in your role. You were hired based on your education, experience, and values. We know that you have the qualifications and capabilities to perform your duties in an exemplary manner. Today, however, our goal is to provide you with the standards by which you will be required to perform those duties. They are part of our mission and our values. They are part of our brand. As a member of the Reliance family, you have an obligation to represent our brand at all times. With every contact, whether it's a patient, a visitor, a vendor, or a community representative, you have the ability to either strengthen or weaken our brand."

"Inside these walls," Dobbins continued, "we all understand that our success and our standing depend on the deepest respect for life. We have a unique responsibility to impact the life of every person who walks through our doors, and I am proud to say that most of our employees are strongly committed to enriching the quality of health and the life of the people we serve. You can do so, as well, by adhering to our brand and implementing the principles that you will learn today as you carry out your duties."

"To explain the principle further, I'd like to share a study which was conducted about how important a brand is to any business or institution. In fact, it's so important that it is the lifeline of success. The point is, we cannot rely solely on the faith that our uniqueness will shine and be evident to those we serve. We can't rest on the laurels that our brand will play out positively with each customer. We have to do something more than rely on the God Only Knows factor. The results of this study provide a fascinating explanation of customer bonding and client relationships.

"In this study, they asked thousands of customers why they bought from whom they bought or why they did business with one business over another. The group was divided into three categories," Phillip explained, before clicking the wireless mouse and once again engaging the monitor, providing the three groups and a brief definition of each.

GROUP ONE: *Features and Benefits*

GROUP TWO: *Relationship*

GROUP THREE: *God Only Knows!*

Phillip went on to explain each of the reasons for

choosing a particular brand over another.

"In the first group, features and benefits were the most important reason for choosing to do business with a particular vendor or organization. Now, a good example of those features and benefits would be 'Two pair of eyeglasses for $99.' That's a feature, as is 0% interest, cash back, 35 miles per gallon, or a money-back satisfaction guarantee. How about the infamous, 'You deserve a break today?' That's a benefit, and those are all reasons why Group One chose to do business with a particular company.

Group Two, on the other hand reported that they selected and stayed with their vendor because they had a specific, unique, or longstanding relationship with them. Their reason is based on a feeling or an emotion. It could be triggered by certain words in their branding which evoke an emotional response, like "Ma" or "Pa." It might also be because they've been around forever and the customer has developed a sense of loyalty toward them. It could be because they have a relationship as a shareholder or the company employs a friend or a relative. Whatever the exact reason, the customer felt a bond or a relationship with the company.

Group Three, however, had no idea why those chose to do business with a particular vendor or what it was that made them stay with that vendor. It's interesting to note that they were the largest group by far. When asked why they buy from a particular company, their answer was, "God Only Knows!," leaving us scratching our heads, wondering just what it is that attracts and keeps customers loyal to their brands.

Now that we know those reasons for choosing a particular brand, let's turn toward the next question posed to the three groups— "Would you switch?" Herein lies the greatest lesson derived from this study. Group One, the group who bought because of features and benefits, said, "Absolutely, we'd switch." What would it take to make them switch? A company who provided the same or better features or benefits. That's all—show them a company who would give them something better, and they're gone."

"The relationship group—Group Two—also said they'd switch, but only if they were presented with the right circumstances."

"Group Three, our God Only Knows group, and again the largest group, had a different answer: "NO WAY!" There was something mysterious, a mojo or bond of sorts, between these folks and their vendor that bonded them like superglue. That mysterious thing is what we call the *God Only Knows* factor (GOK factor). For example, the Ma Bell GOK factor was that emotional connection that we had with "Ma." Knowing that, and knowing that the GOK factor is the only one which was resistant to switching, how can we at Reliance Hospital tap into this group and gain their unbending loyalty? Why do people prefer Reliance Hospital for their medical needs? What is the GOK factor that keeps them happy with the services they receive and their experiences with us? Sure, we have features and benefits, like quality healthcare, affordable services, and for some, a relationship factor that's developed trust and loyalty. But what if another hospital came along that can and does provide all of those things just as well as we do? What's our God Only Knows

Factor that will keep them from switching? Learning about our brand will help you understand that and just how very important it is to the livelihood and survival of Reliance Hospital.

Pausing, Phillip raised his eyes from the notes on the podium to look at his new charges. *Yes*, he thought, *they are still with me*, as he noticed the men and women of various ages focused on him. They all appeared to be concentrating on the presentation—all except one. At the back of the room, stood one man. Impeccably dressed, his back was turned to the room and a cell phone was pressed to his ear.

Ah, yes...there's always one, thought Dobbins. Without fail, he could always pick out the one person who would most likely be guilty of BrandSlaughter. This time, it was Dr. Alexander Barrett, their new chief cardiac surgeon.

Meet BrandSlaughter

After a 15-minute break, the group reassembled and settled in their seats in the auditorium. Phillip turned the mike over to Vivian, so she could introduce the next speaker who would take them into the main theme for today's session.

Duncan Edwards could have been an everyday Joe. An unassuming guy, his gray hair was thinning in the traditional male baldness pattern—a little around the hairline, but even more on top. He didn't look like an executive in the way that most would expect. Absent was the tie, the sport coat, and the polished black wing tips. In their place, was a comfortable brown plaid, button-down shirt, a pair of gently worn khakis, and a pair of dark brown leather loafers which had their share of wear, as well. His gray hair curled just slightly above his ears, which held a pair of reading glasses in place.

He looks exactly like he did when I first met him, Phillip thought to himself. Edwards was a common-sense kind of guy. Not one to beat around the bush, he was quick to bring things out in the open, but in such a way that people weren't offended. That's why Phillip had offered him the position of overseeing the Brand Integrity of Reliance Hospital. He wasn't wrong. People could relate to Duncan—he came across as one of them—non-pretentious and always someone who explained even complex strategies with a simplicity that even a novice could understand. He was a good fit for the job, not only because he had an uncanny way of making people understand the BrandSlaughter concept, but because he was the one who invented it.

"Today," announced Duncan, "you're going to learn how your role at Reliance Hospital represents our brand. What is a brand? What value does it have? And what happens if we fall out of integrity with our brand? Those are some of the questions we're going to pose today as we learn how to prevent ourselves from being implicated for BrandSlaughter."

"Let's get a little informal here. I want today's session to be an atmosphere of give and take, so feel free to pop in when you have a question or a comment, okay? We're a family now, so don't be afraid to speak up."

"I have a question," posed a young lady in the front row. "Okay, first what's your name?"

"Samantha, I mean Sam."

"All right, Sam. What's your question?"

"Well, I've heard the term a couple times, but I still don't think I know what 'BrandSlaughter' is. This might sound stupid, but just what is BrandSlaughter?"

"First, Sam, that's not a stupid question. In fact, it's a very good question, and I'm glad you asked it. You can't possibly know you aren't being a lawful citizen if you don't know what the laws are, right?

"Right," agreed Sam.

"It's also true that you can't know if you're guilty, either directly or indirectly, of BrandSlaughter if you don't know what it is. So, Sam, your question is an important one. BrandSlaughter is when someone is not in integrity with their company's values, or their brand. And when you act or support anything that doesn't build on or feed the brand, the brand slowly dies. The values that a company stands for then cease to exist. When that happens, you are guilty of BrandSlaughter—killing the greatest thing of value that a company— in this instance, our hospital—owns, which is their brand. You can't have it both ways. You are either supporting the brand and in brand integrity, or you are in some way guilty of committing BrandSlaughter."

"Okay, that explains it better," said Sam.

"I think I get it," interjected another man. "It's kind of a fun term that basically says we are not honoring the values that the hospital holds highest. When we do that, we are killing the hospital's image, is that right?"

"Yes," replied Duncan, "but there's more to it than that. When BrandSlaughter is being committed, not only is the company's image in the community destroyed, but internally, employee morale suffers, and ultimately, so does the value we hold highest—quality care for those we serve."

"All because of a company's brand?" asked another gentleman.

"A company's brand is one of its most important assets. Without it, they are no different than any other organization. They have nothing to offer that's different or better than their competitor. When that happens, public perception declines and negative opinions increase. Then people turn elsewhere for their needs, and before you can say 'not guilty,' the business loses its customer base and ceases to exist."

Dr. Barrett, now sitting in the back of the room, spoke up.

"So, Mr. Edwards, let me get this straight. Actually, this concept applies more to other businesses, like retail establishments, more than it does to a hospital. Is that correct?"

"No, Dr. That isn't correct. I use the term 'business' when I teach the BrandSlaughter concept because I want people to understand that the concept is universal. It can be applied to a broad spectrum of industries. We use it faithfully here at Reliance to make sure we are always in brand integrity. But the concept works in manufacturing, sales, social services—you name it."

"Well, as I see it, a hospital takes care of patients. As long as you do that, you should be in brand integrity, so I don't really know how this is applicable to me," replied Dr. Barrett.

"I'm glad you brought up that point, doctor. In reality, your position sounds like it should work, but it doesn't. The reason that it doesn't is because the simple fact that we provide health care for our patients is not enough to keep our brand alive. It is the *manner* in which we provide those services to the people we serve that sets us apart from the rest," answered Duncan.

"Let me put it this way. Levi's blue jeans are sold in thousands of stores across the country, right? They're at

Target, Sears, JC Penney, and dozens of other department stores. They're also sold in independent stores on Main Street and in superstores like Wal-Mart. People know what Levi's jeans are like and no matter where they buy them at, they're still going to get the same pair of jeans. So, what makes them purchase their Levis from one store versus another? Anybody got any ideas?"

"The price." "The location."

"Customer service." "Convenience."

"Exactly," agreed Duncan. "All of those things will have some bearing over the amount of sales of Levis blue jeans that a retail establishment will make. The people who buy Levis will choose to give their business to the store that most closely provides them with the level of satisfaction they demand. A business that doesn't provide them with their jeans in the manner in which their customers expect will lose business and slowly die."

"So, you're saying that Reliance can give the best damn health services in the world, but if we don't do it in the *manner* in which people expect, they'll go elsewhere?" said Dr. Barrett.

"That's precisely what I'm saying," replied Duncan. "But not only do we have to give them the services they want in the manner they expect, but we also have to make sure that we deliver on each and every promise we make. Our brand is our promise and commitment to every person who walks through our doors. If we fail to deliver, we are perpetuating harm to our brand and knowingly or unknowingly, we are guilty of BrandSlaughter. My job here at Reliance is to make sure that doesn't happen."

The BrandSlaughter Police

Phillip observed the exchange quietly from the back of the room. For the most part, it looked like Reliance's new employees were grasping the hospital's brand policy. They were curious, interested, and even intrigued. He especially liked the interaction and inquisitiveness that was displayed—well, by most of them, anyway. For, he couldn't shake a small concern that Dr. Barrett's skepticism was still evident. He knew, though, that Duncan was well equipped to counter any of the surgeon's arguments, no matter what they were. Satisfied that Duncan had everything well under control, he checked his watch, noting that it was time for him to make a quiet exit and prepare for his 10:00 meeting.

At the front of the auditorium, Duncan was prepared to move on. "Are there any other questions before we continue?"

A voice broke through the silence.

"Yes, I have a question. So, how do you know if someone is guilty of BrandSlaughter? Do you have BrandSlaughter police?"

Sporadic laughter spread across the room. Duncan also shared in the light moment, chuckling at the question.

"Well, kind of. Now, don't get me wrong. It's not like we have "police" per se walking around writing tickets and charging people with violating our brand. We don't, and we also don't want anyone to feel that way about our brand policy. There are no arrests or violations which result in severe penalties from BrandSlaughter. Actually, to determine if we are in integrity with our brand, we conduct an audit every six weeks. I am the chief auditor. It's my job not only to identify areas where we aren't in brand integrity, but to find ways to make sure we are."

"A lot of people mistakenly believe that it's a bad thing to be in violation of a policy. Here at Reliance, our audits are conducted from a different perspective. Sure, we love to hear that we are in full compliance and that our brand is alive and well. That's good news. However, the better news is when we can find areas of opportunity where we can be stronger—you know, those areas of our brand that we are undermining. Because when we do, then we know precisely how and where we are committing BrandSlaughter and then we can do something to change it. The fact is, nobody's perfect. We know we aren't perfect. We also know that it's important to identify those areas where we are weak so we can strengthen them. Some people think you should only focus on what's working. Not here at Reliance. Our job is to find out what's not working well, so we can do whatever is necessary to bring those areas back into harmony with our brand."

"So, it's not like your intent is to catch people doing something wrong and discipline them?"

"No, that's not our intent at all. We don't want to single people out in the process—we want to single out areas where we could be better. It makes for a stronger team, a stronger brand, better communication, higher quality of care, and happier employees."

Duncan took the opportunity to continue with this track of thought. "Now, the audit we just spoke about is similar to the audits that most of you are familiar with. Every hospital undergoes a JCAHO audit, right? We know what to expect, what the inspectors are going to check, and if we're smart, we already know if we're in compliance with the regulations, right?"

The group emitted several words of agreement. Everyone knew JCAHO.

"Well," Duncan explained, "that's how the BrandSlaughter audit works. We call it A-B-I, pronounced Abby. It's the Audit of Brand Integrity. I first learned Abby when I was in graduate school. In fact, I still have a copy of the original accreditation form I received from my professor back in the day, believe it or not. When we get a break, I'll run upstairs and see if I can put my hands on it and make copies for y'all."

"So, you conduct this audit just like an accreditation?" piped in a woman wearing nurse scrubs.

"Yes, that's absolutely right. But, I want you to grasp this, so listen closely. Although it is like a hospital accreditation, this is at a higher standard than any other organization can impose upon us. True, it is very much like an accreditation at a university or a hospital, but Abby is bigger and believe it or not, more important because it addresses our highest purpose, which is protecting our biggest asset—our brand. We all know what an asset is, right?"

"It's something of value to a company."

"Yes, exactly," agreed Duncan. "Brand integrity is a huge asset—our number one priority. It's an appreciating asset, though, and I really want you to embrace that concept. It's an asset that we always want to go up in value. We don't want it to depreciate and go down in value. Let me explain. Is a computer an appreciating asset?"

"No."

"How about a car?"

"Are you kidding? A car depreciates the minute you put it into gear."

"That's right," Duncan laughingly agreed. "Well, our brand is different. It can and it does appreciate in value, making it even more important to us every day. Let's take Jim over here," Duncan pointed to a young man to his right. "Now, Jim is an appreciating asset because the longer he is here, the more he knows. He gains more experience. He becomes very valuable to us. Over time, he goes up in value."

"So, we know we have an asset that is appreciating the longer it is with us. Our employees are all appreciating assets, but they aren't the only asset that appreciates. The one other asset we have that truly does appreciate over time is our brand. It goes up in value over time."

"Oh, I think I get it," said Sam.

"Good. It's kind of like Newton's laws of physics. The Law of Brand Integrity says that a brand which is at rest and not fed will die; it won't grow. This means that if we ignore our brand and go on our merry way, we'll eventually starve it and it will cease to exist. Abby, our audit, is the way we tend to our brand, determining precisely what it needs. One might think of it as a checkup. It's like a flower. If you plant it and walk away, it will eventually die from lack of attention, water, light, etc. So, too, will a brand. The purpose of Abby is to find out what the brand needs not only to survive, but to thrive. Is it lacking ingredients which are vital for its growth and survival? What does it need? Where do we focus our efforts? Where are we lacking? What can we do better to make its bloom so exceptional that it would earn the blue ribbon for best of show?"

"So, you're saying that there are no BrandSlaughter police and that you really *want* to find places where brand integrity is weak, rather than aiming for a glowing report?"

"That's right. You see, it's not a crime when you're not in brand integrity. It only becomes a crime when you fail to do anything about it," said Duncan.

Audit of Brand Integrity
Meet "Abby"

Now we're getting into the meat of today's orientation. Ladies and gentlemen, I'd like to introduce you to the most important component of every brand audit, Abby. I call the Audit of Brand Integrity 'Abby' instead of using the acronym ABI for a reason. First, by humanizing the audit, I think people connect to it more. They're less intimidated by it. Also, when you think of it as a name, a person, I think it keeps the process in the proper perspective. The dreaded words "audit" or "accreditation" scare most people, like getting a letter from the IRS, which leaves you shaking in your boots. It's not a 'pass or fail' or a 'do or die' process, but rather an illuminating process that helps us see things which we didn't know were holding us back, so we can fix them. So, our audit is called Abby—she wants to help us and show us the way."

"The beauty of Abby is that she fits in everywhere she goes. She wasn't invented specifically for Reliance Hospital, or even for healthcare organizations, for that matter. Abby is generic and applicable to every industry, business, or organization, regardless if it's manufacturing, retail, food or social service, or even not-for-profit organizations. She's proven herself across the board."

"Let me tell you a little about Abby so you understand her better. Abby has two facets. While her purpose in an organization is to determine where we are in brand integrity and where we need improvement, she focuses on two separate areas: External branding and internal branding. Anyone know the difference?"

"Is external what everyone else can see? Like it's obvious?"

"In a way. External branding is what we say and how we promote ourselves. Internal branding, on the other hand, is how we behave. Until the internal branding process is in place, you shouldn't be advertising your external brand at all."

"Huh?" muttered someone under their breath. Duncan caught the question and expounded.

"Actually, I'm glad that someone just voiced their confusion out loud. It gives me an opportunity to make the concept clearer to you. By the way, that's Abby's purpose—to find areas where we aren't all on the same page and guide us back to where we are supposed to be so we can move forward together."

"Let's say that you're opening a new restaurant—one that specializes in barbeque ribs. Now, your tag line is, 'Bubba's Ribs, the greatest ribs and service you'll find anywhere!' Nothing wrong with that, right?" Duncan paused for effect. "Well, actually there could be something very wrong with that, if Bubba can't deliver on his promise. Now, let's take it a little further and imagine that Bubba is busy preparing for his grand opening. He's ordering food, installing equipment, making phone calls, interviewing prospective employees, placing ads and getting the word out to everyone and anyone that Bubba's Tender Ribs is opening on Friday night. With so much to do, he doesn't have time to adequately train his staff on their brand—part of which is to provide the best darn service around. Along comes Friday night and the place is packed, Bubba's grinning from ear to ear, and then, the rug is pulled out from under his feet. The customers aren't happy. They're complaining left and right about the slow service and the fact that their orders are getting mixed up. Bubba underprepared for such a huge crowd and people had to wait for 30, 45 minutes to get a table. The disgruntled customers are making his servers uneasy and upset. That's hardly a recipe for great service, is it? Well, because Bubba proclaimed to the world that his restaurant offered great service and he didn't deliver, he's lost the stamp of approval from his customer base. He couldn't deliver what he promised. What was Bubba's mistake?"

"Bubba failed to make sure that he could actually do what he promised in his ads."

"That's right. Bubba's external brand was what he said and the way he promoted his restaurant. His internal brand is how he actually behaves or executes that brand. He didn't have his internal brand in place. He hadn't sufficiently trained his staff or prepared his business to deliver what they promised, regardless of the circumstances. In this case, Bubba was out of brand integrity because he couldn't deliver the outstanding service he advertised. The moral of Bubba's demise: Don't embarrass yourself by declaring how great you are and then not be able to deliver. Don't be inconsistent with what you say and what you do. It's a conflict between your internal brand and your external brand, and it's the kiss of death for many a business."

"How would Abby help in that instance?" interjected one young man.

"Good question, I'm glad you asked," replied Duncan. "Before Bubba opened his restaurant, he needed to make sure that he was in brand integrity. Even more, he needed to verify that his employees understood the importance of their brand and that they were in harmony with it. Bubba failed to do that, and even though he might have had the best ribs this side of the Rockies, he couldn't deliver to the public. How could he have used Abby to prevent this BrandSlaughter? First, Abby would have provided him with a checklist of critical items that must be in place across the board before they opened. The audit would have given him insight into where they weren't prepared or in harmony with their brand. They could have even held a trial grand opening, doing a run-through of several different scenarios, and practicing the proper way to handle those different situations. When the employees knew what to do and how to respond to different circumstances in a way that was in full integrity with their brand, Bubba would have had reasonable assurance that they could deliver on their promises, regardless of the circumstances. The bonuses? His customers would have been impressed with the way they handled a packed house. Rather than being frustrated, his employees would have taken pride in the way they handled a difficult situation. And Bubba would have a business that would thrive and grow, instead of dying on the bloom the day he planted it."

"Was it all Bubba's fault? What if he had hired a couple employees who had a bad day? What if they didn't deliver?"

"A-Ha!" Duncan came to life. "Beautiful question! Why should Bubba fail because he had a couple bad apples? Well, let's go back to the BrandSlaughter philosophy: You are either supporting the brand and in brand integrity or you are guilty of BrandSlaughter—either directly or by association. Abby shows us that whether you are directly involved in the offense of BrandSlaughter or not, as the leader of the organization you are complacent, or guilty by association. I understand that Bubba might not have been the one who never smiled, who heaved a big sigh when someone asked for more ketchup, or who delivered an order to the wrong table. But he is guilty of BrandSlaughter to the second degree. It's his responsibility that everyone in the organization is in brand integrity because the brand has value. Abby shows us that when you put the brand in the hands of your employees, you make the decision that they know how the brand works and how to implement it. They know how to nurture it and take care of it. That's Bubba's responsibility—to make sure his entire organization understands, values, and represents the brand at all times."

"It's like placing a child in a daycare center. You call around, looking for someone to take care of your kid from 9 to 5, five days a week. You finally find someone, drop your child off, and go to work. Now, what if something happened to that child while you were at work? What if they wandered off or maybe they weren't being watched closely and got hurt? Whose fault is it? Sure, the daycare worker was negligent, but is he or she the only one? We know it's not the child's fault, but shouldn't the person who chose to leave the child in the hands of that particular caregiver shoulder some of the responsibility? By putting the child in that daycare, the parent chose to separate their responsibility, and the daycare worker agreed to

accept that responsibility. So, although the parent didn't harm their child, their actions and decisions played a role in the outcome. Bubba's actions, or lack thereof, made him guilty of BrandSlaughter in the second degree— especially if he didn't call attention to the BrandSlaughter and pull his staff into integrity right away."

"Abby's job is to make sure that all areas from the top down and the bottom up are in compliance with the internal and external brand. Do what you promise you're going to do, and promise only what you are certain you can and will deliver. Find out your strengths and take advantage of them. Identify your weaknesses and work together diligently to bring them into harmony and integrity with what you say, how you promote yourself, and how you deliver on your promises. Bubba failed to do that."

Sam again spoke up, catching on to the concept nicely. "So, it's like false advertisement, right?"

"In many ways, Sam, it is. If you say you're going to do something, do it. If you say you're going to give the best gall-darned service in town, then make sure you actually give people the best gall- darned service. Otherwise, you're going to have some unsatisfied, angry customers, and your brand will be deemed worthless. It will die, just as quickly as if you pulled the plug and said do-not-resuscitate. Speaking of do not resuscitate, I think we're all ready for some sustenance. After our lunch break, we'll get into Abby and the audit process in more detail and I'll clue you in on the different areas Abby checks to make sure we are in brand integrity—and what actions we take if we aren't. For now, you can take your free lunch tickets to the cafeteria and treat yourself to the salad bar or one of today's specials. Take this opportunity to look around and observe ways that Reliance is or is not in integrity, and we'll talk about it when we return in an hour."

The Checklist

Duncan turned off the overhead monitor, checked to make sure he wasn't forgetting anything, and quickly exited the auditorium. If he was lucky, he could make it upstairs in time to find his copy of the original audit he'd been given in grad school and give it to his assistant to copy before she went to lunch. If not, he'd do it himself, but he had promised Phillip he'd stick his head in the door and join the disaster drill meeting that had started half an hour ago.

As he passed the front entrance, he looked out the glass doors just as a black Mercedes convertible was pulling out of a parking space near the door reserved for surgeons. Eying Walker, who was most likely en route to the disaster meeting, he quickly caught up to him. "Hey, Walker, do you know who owns the black Mercedes convertible that was parked in the surgeons' lot?"

"Sure do," answered Walker. "That's the new cardiac surgeon who's in your orientation today, Dr. Barrett."

"Hmmm, interesting," replied Duncan.

Continuing up the stairs to his office, Duncan thought about Dr. Barrett. Was he anti-social? Did he think he was too good to eat with the other new employees? *Maybe*, thought Duncan, *he has an appointment during the lunch hour. I should give him the benefit of the doubt.* Then, forgetting all about Dr. Barrett, he walked through his office door, went to the bottom drawer of his filing cabinet and pulled out the audit form. *Well, it's seen better days*, he observed, *but at least I can deliver on my promise.*

Looking toward his assistant's desk, he noticed he was too late, so he walked down the hall, put the paper in the copy machine, pressed in a sufficient number to make sure he had enough copies, plus a few extra for good measure, and set off to the CEO's conference room.

Phillip Dobbins was in the middle of delegating responsibilities for Reliance's upcoming disaster drill. During the last five years, it had become tradition to hold annual mock drills to ensure the staff was prepared to handle various potential disaster or calamities. Iowa, after all, was in tornado territory, and they'd also had their share of major floods which had caused loss of property and life. Dobbins' goal was to make sure they were ready to handle whatever might come their way, from workplace disasters to environmental hazards.

"Oh, Duncan, glad you were able to make it," Dobbins nodded, acknowledging Duncan as he pulled out a chair. "I asked you to stop by today because I think this

disaster drill is a good opportunity for you to audit our response systems in the event of a community emergency. Do you think you could oversee the process and use Abby as a checklist to make sure we're in brand integrity under those circumstances?"

"I'm certain I can. As a matter of fact, that's a very good time to ensure that our brand is being integrated under extreme conditions. From what I've found, those are times when, in our haste to respond to many demands and emergency situations, we unknowingly fall out of brand integrity. Unfortunately, those are times when it's also most important to stay within our integrity. Should be interesting to see the results of the audit when we're responding to situations beyond our control."

"Like Bubba and the packed house," Dobbins laughed.

"Hey, don't knock Bubba—he's a good example of what can happen if you're not in harmony with your brand."

"I know. I know," Dobbins agreed. "Just having some fun with you. Let's hope Reliance doesn't suffer the same results Bubba did, though."

"We won't," Duncan assured him. "Because Abby's purpose is to pull us back into integrity if we fall to the wayside. Bubba's problem was that he didn't even have Abby to save him or his tender ribs. If that's all, I've got to grab a quick bite and return to the auditorium. If it's okay, I'll write up a proposal on how we can implement Abby in the drill and have that on your desk by the end of the week?"

"Sure," replied Dobbins. "Take your time. By the way, how's the orientation going? When I left, you were explaining the importance of Abby to our new surgeon."

"Well, everything's going pretty smoothly. But when I left, so did your surgeon. Hopefully, he'll be back after lunch. I'll let you know."

Do No Harm

Grabbing his photocopies, Duncan sat them on a table in the break room and pulled a salad out of the refrigerator. It was his typical lunch, salad and a couple crackers, chased by a Diet Coke. He liked to eat light, saving his major meal of the day for supper, when he could actually sit down and eat at his leisure. Ten minutes later, he was on his way back to the auditorium, ready to dive into the afternoon part of the session.

After turning the equipment back on, Duncan leaned on the podium, watching as the group sprinkled in. Some were alone, others walked through the doors in groups of two, three, or more. He noticed they were making small talk, and some were even laughing. *That's good*, he thought. *Camaraderie in the workplace keeps morale up and inspires teamwork.*

A few minutes later, Duncan scanned the crowd. Glancing at his watch, he noted that it was time to get started, especially since it looked like just about everybody had returned and taken their seats. The only person who was unaccounted for was Dr. Barrett.

After clearing his throat to get their attention, Duncan once again reminded everyone in the auditorium that they should silence their cell phones and put them away. A few blips and beeps later, they were ready to get started.

"As I promised, I've made copies of the generic audit I received in grad school. I've placed copies on the table at the back of the room. You're invited to stop by and pick a copy up before you leave today. Now, let's move along. Where were we?" he asked, pausing before remembering.

"Oh, when you went to lunch, I asked you to be observant and look for signs that we are or are not in brand integrity. Did anyone see anything they'd like to share?"

A hand shot up, belonging to a gentleman in an aisle seat on the left side of the room.

"Yes," Duncan invited.

"I noticed several places where the hospital's mission statement is posted for the public's viewing."

"That's part of our external brand. Our mission statement is our promise and dedication to all who walk through our doors, stating precisely what we intend to deliver at all times and the manner in which we'll do so. Anyone else?"

"Well, I don't know if this is what you're looking for, really, but in the cafeteria, I paid attention to how the employees treated us. I have to commend them. They were friendly and helpful. Some even made recommendations when we asked what was good today. One of them even stopped cleaning a table to help a guy using a walker carry his tray."

"Those are good examples. They reveal how each department is in harmony with our brand in different ways. In the cafeteria, they might be focused on customer service, quality, appearance, efficiency, and on eliminating waste. In another area, like in Radiology, they might maintain brand integrity through some of the same things, like customer service, appearance, and efficiency, but they could also focus on other factors, like productivity and accuracy. That's how Abby works; regardless of each department's purpose, they all have responsibilities to build our brand to the base they serve."

"For that reason, the employees we hire are an integral and vital part of our brand. Without our employees, we couldn't address the needs of our patients, vendors, or the community. You've all been chosen for a reason. Naturally, we feel you are qualified for the job which you've been hired to do, but most importantly, we feel that you are a good representative for our brand. A part of learning how to be in brand integrity is knowing how to recognize when you are guilty of BrandSlaughter. So, let's look at a few examples."

"When you are hired, we give you certain rules to live by. Just about every organization does. One of the most important rules is todo no harm. Do no harm to our reputation. Do no harm to our patients. Do no harm to our accreditation status. Do no harm to our vendors. Do no harm to our brand. Well, let's look at a fictitious scenario and see if you can determine whether any harm is being done."

Leaving the podium, Duncan slowly paced across the front of the room. "In the hospital," he began, "when we perform a test and find out that someone has a low white blood cell count, you don't penalize them for that, right? You rectify it."

"Well, just like when a patient's blood count is out of the norm, out of integrity with what their body requires to function at its best, when we find out we are out of integrity with our brand, we find out what we can do to reduce the issue and its impact on our hospital."

"Here's an example. Several children are crying in the lab as they're getting their blood drawn. They're fearful of the procedure, like many kids, and adults, I must add, are. Now, the lab technicians don't know that these cries can be heard in the waiting room, where other children are waiting their turn. Hearing these cries, those kids are getting nervous, too. They're anxious, scared, and as a result, they are tensing their muscles. What happens when you tense your muscles before you're injected with a needle?"

"It hurts a lot more."

"That's right. So every time a child cries, the level of anxiety in the waiting room rises. Those kids waiting their turn tense up even more, so when it comes time for their needle prick, they guarantee that the experience wouldn't be a good one. Does that affect our brand?"

"Not really," interjected a young woman, "because you can't control the fact that children are afraid of shots."

"No," agreed Duncan, "we cannot entirely control that. Although many nurses and lab techs most certainly wish we could. However, there are some things we can control. We can control the noise control by installing soundproof barriers. We can control the anxiety of the children by taking measures to calm them down and make them feel comfortable. If we say we provide quality healthcare in a caring environment, but by being in our environment, children feel fear, we aren't entirely in brand integrity. This really did happen here at Reliance. What did we do? First, we did install additional sound barriers. Then, we offered staff training on ways to reduce stress levels in children in such situations. By taking a few extra minutes to talk to the child, calm and comfort them, and earn their trust, we were able to reduce the amount of tension significantly. This is an area we revisit ever six weeks as we explore even more ways we can stay within our brand integrity."

"So, it's our job to find ways to lessen the impact that fear has on the public's perception of the hospital?" asked Sam.

"It's your job, my job, Abby's job—it's everyone's job—even the cafeteria worker who voluntarily lends a hand to someone who needs help. Fear is natural in a health institution. People are sick, injured, and sometimes, they're scared. But we don't want people to sense fear when they walk in the door. We prefer that the first impression they get of our environment is the caring manner in which we carry out our duties, providing our patients and their families with assurance and peace of mind. The fear is still there, and we know we have to address it. So we find ways to reduce the fear and increase what does work. Then we celebrate the fact that we are in integrity with our brand."

"How do we recognize when we aren't in brand integrity? In the example I just gave, I pointed out that the lab technicians didn't know that people in the waiting room could hear the children crying. So, how did they know what was wrong and that it needed to be fixed? Abby told them. On one of my audits, I heard the shrieks and wails of frightened little kids, and as I walked through the waiting room, I noticed the obvious tension among the other children as their parents frantically tried to calm them down. The lab techs didn't know what was going on in the waiting room, and they had no idea that the crying was contributing to the anxiety in the patients who were waiting. It was noted during the audit—we sat down and came up with various solutions, implemented the best ones, and now we recheck them regularly to make sure they're still effective."

"I'm starting to see how this audit or accreditation, as you called it, could actually make employees' jobs easier. At first, I thought it was going to be a lot of rules and regulations and paperwork, which would have been a headache," said a young man.

"Thanks for point that out. While we say that BrandSlaughter is a crime, it's not a police investigation. It's nothing more than a tool that is designed to make everyone's job easier and our entire operation more productive and functional. In fact, we don't punish anyone when they are out of brand integrity; however, we always celebrate when we're back in integrity, I assure you."

"You mean like the Baldrige award?"

"Exactly. Baldrige awards those who are role models in providing performance excellence. The Audit of Brand Integrity is very similar. Abby auditors also award excellence, whether it's in medical expertise, productivity, care, quality, appearance, or efficiency."

"I think my husband's company does the same thing," a woman announced. "He works in a chemical plant, and they have teams made up of the production crews who are asked to find ways to increase production, while lowering costs. When their proposals are implemented, each member of the team receives a bonus—or an award as you call it—giving them one percent of the annual cost savings. It might not sound like much, but if their idea saves $200,000, each member of the team gets a bonus of $2,000. Believe me, that comes in handy."

"I'm really glad you shared that," Duncan said. "Incentives are a good way to bring an organization further into brand integrity. When efficiency and productivity both increase, the brand grows. Employees are inspired to do even more when they're rewarded for their efforts to make that happen."

"You know, talking about efficiency and productivity reminds me of the Tater Tot story."

"Go ahead, Dennis," invited Duncan. "Share the Tater Tot story with us."

"Well, as I remember it, back in the early days when frozen food was taking off, the Griggs brothers bought a company and called it Ore-Ida. I'm sure you've all heard of them, right? Well, they didn't believe in waste. I guess you could say part of their brand was efficiency, and of course, productivity. So, anyway, they had a lot of scraps left over after they cut the fries. Rather than throwing them away and having waste, they sold them to farmers for feed. But the bad part was, they weren't making much money doing that. I guess it was something, but they didn't think it was they were getting the best return for the scraps. So, they put their heads together and found a way to use the scraps in a product, which they could sell for a lot more than they were getting from the farmers. By shredding the potato scraps even more and rolling them together and frying them, they invented a new product, which we know today as Tater Tots."

"Thank you, Dennis. The Tater Tot story is a great example of how a business can increase efficiency. The owners of Ore-Ida certainly wanted to increase productivity, but they also wanted to decrease waste. Tater Tots gave them a way to do both at the same time, making them more efficient and productive. Plus, nobody can deny that Tater Tots did wonders for their brand," added Duncan. "But before any of these measures can be implemented, someone has to identify the areas which are out of integrity with the brand. That's all Abby is designed to do—to find out where a business can be more cost-conscious, efficient, productive, or caring—so our good employees can work with us to make our establishment better for us and for everyone who walks in the door." Almost if on cue, the back door opened, and in walked Dr. Barrett, 45 minutes late for the afternoon session.

"The F Word"

Duncan made a mental note of Dr. Barrett's tardiness to the session, but he didn't let the interruption interfere with his agenda. For the most part, the group was attentive, and he noted that in many ways, they were more interactive than some he'd seen in the past.

"Now that you understand a little about BrandSlaughter and Abby, I want to talk about how it will affect you as you fulfill your daily responsibilities here at Reliance. I've already said it before and can't stress it enough, our employees are our brand. They are the conveyors of our brand to our patients, the public, the community, and to our vendors and service providers. Without you, we simply could not meet our standards and fulfill our promise to the community and the people we serve."

"Our BrandSlaughter audit checks to make sure that all jobs are being done, but more importantly, we're insuring that they're done in a manner which supports our brand. In addition, we're specifically looking to find ways that we're not supporting our brand in the best way possible. Usually, that would be a bad thing, right? Well here at Reliance, it's a good thing. It's our assurance that we continually growing and improving. We could sweep problems or difficulties under the rug, but that won't get rid of them. They'll always be there, and someday, somebody will lift that rug and we'll have to deal with them. Our philosophy is to deal with it right away, as soon as we find it. Then we know that the issue is addressed and won't present itself again."

"Now, you were specifically selected as one of our

employees because we believe that you have the qualities and the qualifications that support our brand. The folks here at Reliance believed that you would represent our brand in a way that would breathe new life into it every time you stepped in the door. We could have hired anybody, but we chose you because you most closely mirror the qualities we believe are most important in our employees."

"Before I go any further, does anyone know what the most common cause is for relieving a person of their duties within the first six months of their employment?"

"You mean what the main reason is that people are fired?" asked Sam.

"Yes, if you want to call it that," Duncan said, looking around as he waited for an answer.

"Okay," he added. "I'll tell you since you don't seem to know. The most common reason people are let go within the first six months of their employment is, "You are not a good fit." You're not a good fit for our company or our business. What does that mean?"

"It means that the boss doesn't like them," offered a lady in the back row.

Chuckling, Duncan said, "Well, it could, I guess. But you know, not being a good fit doesn't have to mean that the boss doesn't like you. In fact, the boss could love you, thinking that you're upbeat and happy, just a swell person to be around. You motivate everybody and keep them laughing and jovial all day long. But, no matter how bubbly your personality is, you still might not be a good fit. Think about it…What if you were the office clown, but you worked for a funeral home? Now, that's not a good fit."

The comment resulted in laughter, but Duncan thought he'd made his point.

"As you can see, being a good fit can be a critical factor in an employer-employee relationship. It's one of the most important F words there is. What it basically means, is that the way you conduct yourself as you represent our organization is a good fit to our brand, not to your boss. Your supervisor and you could have totally different personalities, but you weren't hired to complement your supervisor. You were hired to complement and represent our brand. That's where you're a good fit. Any questions?"

Sporadic 'no's' broke through the silence, so Duncan continued on.

"Now, let me give you a doctor-patient example of how being a good fit with our brand works. This is hypothetical, so don't think I'm giving away any juicy gossip here and divulging top-secret HR files, okay?"

"Let's say that we just hired a Dr. Smith to our staff. Dr. Smith is a brilliant doctor; he's a left-brained, analytical scientist. He can recite a medical encyclopedia backwards if he wants to. But there's a problem. After we hired Dr. Smith and celebrated the fact that we recruited this remarkable medical gem, we found that Dr. Smith has a terrible bedside manner. He's gruff, short-spoken, and dismissive when he talks to patients. He has little patience when they ask him to explain things differently or in more detail. And when they're at their most vulnerable, or concerned, he invokes little or no compassion toward them. He views his job as providing medical care, and that's all."

"I've known doctors like that," somebody interjected from the left side of the room.

"I think we all have," agreed Duncan. "Seriously, though, not to put doctors down because I know many, many great ones, but what is this doctor doing wrong? How is he not representing our brand?"

"He's not caring."

"He doesn't seem interested in the patient, just in the symptoms."

"Dr. Smith is one cold-hearted guy."

"Well, all of the above," replied Duncan. "Sure, he's a cold- hearted guy, but he justifies that by saying that the patient isn't looking for a new "BFF," but rather someone who will accurately diagnose them and treat them. And, I might add, Dr. Smith does do that. So, is he wrong?"

"Not really, but like you said, he might not be a good fit," spoke Dennis.

"That's true, Dennis. He might be doing an exceptional job at treating his patients and providing them with his valuable medical expertise, but he's not seeing the whole picture. At Reliance, we know that when our patients have a good, open relationship with their doctor, they're more likely to communicate important information to them. When they have good rapport with their medical team, they're also much more likely to follow doctor's orders. They comply with pre and post-op instructions more completely. And as a result, they heal better and much more quickly. That's what Dr. Smith doesn't understand."

"So, do you fire him?" asked Sam.

"In many places, Sam, Dr. Smiths would be terminated because they are "not a good fit," answered Duncan, emphasizing the phrase by making quote marks in the air with his fingers. "But at Reliance, we believe in our employees and our competent medical staff. In the event that we find that one of them is not in brand integrity, which in this case, is to provide quality care in a caring environment, we prefer to approach it from the angle of solving the problem, not ridding ourselves of it. How do we do that? We try to prevent the problem before it happens by assigning each of our employees with a mentor, someone who has already familiarized themselves fully with our brand and represents the brand in integrity. If that should fail or if we find that the individual is not in harmony with our brand down the road, we pull them back into harmony again through mentorship, having them work directly with someone who excels in the area in which they need improvement. Our goal is to improve, always to improve—never to punish. It's the best solution for our brand, our patients, and our employees.

What's Your Job?

When you all report to your department for your first day of work, you'll receive a list of the duties and responsibilities assigned to your position. Now, those duties are unique to your job and your trade. What applies to a dietitian won't necessarily apply to medical transcriptionist, a security officer, or a radiologist. That's a given, right? But there are some duties and responsibilities that are universal here at Reliance, and I want to cover a few of them today."

"Have you ever heard the age-old line, 'That's not my job?' Everyone's heard that at one time or another. It's an old fallback for some employees, and it makes most bosses cringe when they hear it. There are some things that indeed are your job, no matter what your job is. Most of those things are connected directly to our brand."

"We know that looks aren't everything, but we also know that first impressions are everything. For that reason, and for sanitary purposes, too, our physical facility demands that every employee keep a clean, well kept and organized workplace. Not only in your own personal work area, such as your desk, but also in the entire hospital. Every employee is expected to do their part to keep our hospital neat and presentable. Cleanliness is everyone's job—you can call it the first C in your universal duties. Inside and out, the manner in which the public perceives our facility is their first impression of us and the standards we insist upon."

"For example, I don't know if any of you saw Walker Briggs standing outside the front entrance this morning.

Walker is the Chief of Security here at Reliance, and that's his morning post. You can't miss him. He's out there every morning, come rain or shine, keeping a watchful eye on every person and vehicle that comes onto our grounds. If you don't know Walker, you will, because he knows every employee in this hospital and somehow makes it a point to personally speak to each of them every day.

Now, this morning, I noticed Walker standing guard, as usual, and as his eye passed across, he noticed a piece of litter in the lily bed next to the doors, so he sauntered over, bent down, picked it up and disposed of it in the nearest trash can. Walker could have said, "That's not my job," and waited for the grounds crew to come along and clean it up, but he didn't. That's because Walker knows our brand, he promotes it, and he contributes to it. If he sees something that's out of place, he'll put it back. He takes pride in the appearance of our hospital and the image we convey to the community."

"Another universal responsibility that Abby checks for is communication. Abby likes people who communicate. If there's a problem, Abby wants you to tell someone about it. If there is something that needs to be shared within your department, by all means, communicate it. Above all, Abby wants you to communicate not only within your own department, but with other departments. The right hand likes to know what the left hand is doing. Only then, can they work together and operate at full efficiency and productivity. By working together and communicating, we form the teamwork of a well-oiled machine and avoid delays, confusion, and the other C word: Chaos."

"Here are a couple more C words for you: Caring and Compassion. In everything you do at Reliance, these words are the foundation of the way you carry out your expertise and duties. Yes, you are expected to provide quality, if not exceptional care, to every patient who enters our doors, but you're also expected to be caring and compassionate with every person you address. It could be a vendor who is bringing in free samples. It could be the Xerox repair guy, or it might be the UPS man in brown. It could be someone calling to confirm their lab tests, or a grandparent visiting their newborn grandson for the first time. Every person you meet and communicate with, from the patient who is terminally ill to the six-year-old getting stitches, is to be treated with care and compassion."

"That's not always easy to do in a stressful environment, and believe me, sometimes a hospital can be stressful. But it's always necessary. You are representing our brand with every person you make contact with, and every action and word on your part represents all of us and what we believe in. You attitude and behavior to our patients, their families, our vendors, and your co-workers significantly impacts everyone's experiences and their perception of Reliance and what we do."

"If you do your job well and always remember the four C's, you'll be in harmony with our brand most of the time. But when just one of those things is neglected, something, somewhere will be negatively impacted. That's what we want to avoid."

"Now, I'm going to give you a break and set you lose on your own for a while. If you haven't already picked up a copy of the generic Abby audit, go to the back door and get one. Then, I want you to break up into a couple of groups and walk around our hospital. Familiarize yourself with our facility and have a little fun conducting your own Abby audit. When you see something that's obviously in brand integrity, make note of it, and if you see something that's not in harmony with our brand, that's even better. Write it down. Now, go take a short break, then explore. Before you leave for the day, bring your audit notes back to the table. Any questions?"

There was no response as everyone rose out of their chairs, stretching their legs. "Okay, then," Duncan finished. "It's been a pleasure to be with you today and introduce you to Reliance's brand. Welcome to Reliance Hospital, and good luck to each of you."

As Duncan spoke, he noticed Dr. Barrett walking toward the back door, briefcase in hand. Hurriedly, he picked up his pace to catch up with him.

"Dr. Barrett," he called out.

The doctor stopped, turning around to face Duncan.

"I wanted to take an opportunity to personally introduce myself. I've heard a lot of good things about you and can tell you that we're excited to have your expertise on staff here at Reliance."

"Thank you, now, I'm in a rush, so if you'll excuse me," answered the doctor.

"You aren't going to join the others in a tour of the facilities?" inquired Duncan.

"I don't have time for that. Frankly, this whole day has been a waste of my time. I was hired to fix hearts and save lives, not to listen to a bunch of nonsense about brands and picking up trash. I get paid to do my job and you get paid to do yours. My job has nothing to do with saving or killing a brand, or BrandSlaughter or whatever you call it. My job is to save people."

"Well, I beg to disagree with you, Dr. In order to do your job and be at your best, you need the cooperation and teamwork of a lot of people and departments. Reliance's brand will ensure that you get that level of cooperation, but if you aren't in integrity with our brand, you'll risk losing it. Our image and reputation in the community directly mirror each other in the long run. Brand integrity starts from the top down."

"Like I said before, that's not my job," Dr. Barrett sternly replied. "Now if you'll excuse me, I have better things to do."

Duncan watched as he turned on his heels and walked out the door.

"Someday, doctor," he whispered, "you're going to take those words back. No man is an island. Someday, you're gonna find out just how much you need our brand and the full cooperation of our employees. I guarantee it."

An Appetite for Excellence

Phillip Dobbins tucked a few folders into his briefcase and snapped it shut before turning off his computer and heading out the door. Tonight his wife had her weekly chef's class, an interest she dearly loved. Admittedly, Phillip loved it, too, for she often whipped up some pretty enticing and unique dishes for their family. Jill usually did the carpools, picking up Nathan and Sara from baseball, dance, or whatever activity they were involved in at the time. But, on Mondays, Phillip got to wear the chaperone's hat, so he kept a close eye on the time to make sure he got to the baseball field to pick up their eight-year-old son by 6:00.

En route to the park was a corner café, a long-standing mom and pop diner that catered to families in the area. The atmosphere was clean, but nothing special. There was no particular theme or gimmicks on the walls—just white laminate tables surrounded by chairs upholstered in red vinyl. Yet, the place was usually packed. The special of the day changed with the calendar date, and you never knew just what was on the menu until you got there. It was a unique place that Phillip and Jill had found one afternoon after doing some holiday shopping. From time to time, they'd returned, and along the way, had found the true delicacy of Blue's Café—their pies. While it was true that you never knew what was on the menu until you looked at the neon board on the wall, there was one thing you could count on—this place had the best pie he'd ever tasted. As had become his tradition on Mondays, Phillip swung into the parking lot to pick up the family's dessert for the night.

After debating for a second, Phillip chose the peach over the banana crème pie, and satisfied, climbed in the car to pick up their son. The team was in their post practice huddle when he pulled up, so he sat and waited in the car until he heard, "Go, team!" and then popped open the trunk. After throwing in his bat bag and helmet, he made sure his son buckled up and headed home.

"How was practice?" Phillip asked.

The ride home was filled with small talk about baseball and school until they pulled in the garage ten minutes later. Instructing his son to put his gear away, Phillip went inside to check on Sara, knowing already that she was probably in her room doing her homework or talking on the phone—probably both. Then, he flipped through the mail, noting nothing of interest, tossed it on the counter, and read Jill's note to see what was for supper and her usual instructions for warming it up.

Beef tenderloin, egg noodles, and a mushroom sauce...*hmm, that sounds pretty good*, Phillip thought as he removed it from the refrigerator and set the oven timer for 30 minutes. Then he took the peach pie out of the box and placed it alongside the casserole dish on the oven rack so it would be warm, too. *There's nothing better than a homemade pie, fresh from the oven*, he thought.

While dinner was warming, he tossed a salad and set the table. The kids came downstairs and somehow managed to eat while talking a mile a minute, and then went back to their homework. He knew he'd have to check on Nathan, who probably would get distracted by a video game before long, but everything was fine.

He grabbed a cup of coffee, a piece of pie, and one of the folders from his briefcase and sat down in his recliner. The mock drill they were planning was a large one, encompassing several fire and police departments, as well as one of the town's biggest industrial manufacturers, where the pretend disaster would take place. It would require a thorough review of their communication abilities, trauma units, personnel, and their physical capacity. He had another hour or so before Jill came home, so he sat down to work out the particulars. But before he did, he put his fork into his pie and took a generous bite, thinking that as long as they continued to bake pies like this, Blue's Café would have his business.

Valuable Input

Duncan was greeted by his two dogs, Niko, a three-year-old pure white husky with clear blue eyes, and Lassie, the border collie mix they'd had since the kids lived at home. After taking them out, he checked the messages on the machine, threw the morning coffee cups in the dishwasher, and flipped over the bag of steaks which were marinating in the refrigerator. After washing a couple potatoes and wrapping them in foil, he tossed them in the oven.

With the kids grown and gone, Duncan and his wife made it a point to eat a nice dinner together every night. Because their shifts overlapped, they didn't have that much time together. Lynne was an LPN at the hospital, and her shift ended at 7 p.m., so Duncan usually was in charge of cooking the last meal of the day, while Lynne took care of the laundry and the cleaning in the morning before she went to work. That's why Duncan usually ate a light lunch—he preferred to relax over a nice, leisurely meal with his wife and talk about their day.

Duncan, too, had brought home some work from the office, if you could call it that. He liked to think of it as homework or curiosity. The Abby audits from the orientation were in his brown leather briefcase on the countertop, and given the interest the new employees had expressed during the day, he was just as interested, if not more, to see how they'd filled out their audit forms. Throughout the years, he'd found that he could tell a lot about an employee based on their first impression of the hospital. Some were obviously non-committal, checking the same box all the way down, meets expectations, meets expectations, meets expectations. Those are the ones who usually left the comments sections blank, as well. Nothing to see there. But it was those who really took the audit to heart that opened his eyes to things that, admittedly, sometimes he failed to see. Duncan was the first to admit that if you looked at something day after day, you failed to notice the small details. Sometimes, the audits by the new employees placed fresh eyes on the things that might otherwise go unnoticed.

Lighting the grill, Duncan took the dogs out with him while he seared the steaks. Medium, with just a hint of pink in the middle, was how they liked them, and he was a pro at cooking them just right. He found grilling a great way to unwind after being cooped up in the hospital all day. Breathing in the fresh air and watching their pets run across their two-acre rural lot was one of the most enjoyable parts of his day. So much so, that it wasn't unusual to catch Duncan flipping a steak, pork chop, or chicken breast in the dead of winter. Unlike most people, he found it exhilarating.

Satisfied that the sirloins had reached the peak of their perfection, he took them off the grill, just as Lynne pulled into the drive. Leaving her to grab the dogs, he went inside and put the food on the table, poured a glass of wine for each of them so they could breathe for a minute, and went into the back hallway to feed the pups.

They made their usual small talk during dinner. Lynne had talked to their daughter who was a senior at Iowa State, and was excited to announce that she was coming home to visit for the weekend. Duncan talked about the orientation, bringing her up to speed on some of the hospital's new hires.

"Did you know Nanette's back again? It was good to see her face among the group."

"That's nice. What did you think of the new Chief of Cardiac Surgery?" Lynne asked. This was an area of concern for Lynne, and Duncan knew it. She had just transferred to the cardiac unit last year, and he had gotten the impression there was some apprehension about the new chief, given his impressive credentials and admittedly even more impressive reputation for being one of the best, but most demanding, heart surgeons in the country.

For two reasons, Duncan was unwilling to say anything negative about Dr. Barrett. First, he didn't want to unnecessarily cause his wife any anxiety. Secondly, he couldn't honestly say that he had an opportunity to assess the doctor well enough to express an opinion about what kind of supervisor he would be and how he would run their cardiac unit or treat their employees. So, rather than saying something he might regret later, he chose to toe the line.

"I don't know, Lynne. In all honesty, I didn't see much of him, but we did get a chance at the end of the day to exchange introductions," he said.

"Oh, I was hoping you'd be able to tell me something that would help me know a little more about him before we meet, but that's okay, I guess. No news is good news. I'd rather hear nothing than something bad."

With that, Duncan turned the conversation toward safe

topics, asking her to remember to pick up butter and another 20-pound bag of dog food at the market tomorrow. It seemed those dogs never got full, they laughed, as they looked over at the boys who were waiting patiently to go outside once again.

After everyone was settled in for the night, Duncan turned the TV on to the nightly news and opened his Abby folder. There were quite a few audits, something which he was glad to see. But would he be glad to read what they had to say?

Flipping through the stack, he immediately eliminated half a dozen of the obvious ones—the meets expectations checked consistently for every single area. They wouldn't be helpful to him. He wanted to see where they exceeded expectations, but above all, where they needed improvement. Those were the audits that piqued his interest.

As a measure of confidentiality and a way to encourage the new hires to provide an honest assessment, the initial Abby audit was voluntary, and they were told not to put their names on them. Their responses were solely for learning purposes, nothing more. What Duncan hoped to gain from them was the impression first-time visitors got when they walked through the hospital. And often he did.

In the past, each group had brought something unique to his attention. Today's group was no different. Several indicated they were impressed with the cleanliness and the décor of the facilities, and a few thought a couple areas were overcrowded, which was something that the administration and the Board were already addressing.

There were a couple that commented on the friendliness of the staff they'd met, which was always nice to see. But there were a few that caught his eye. Giving it further review, he could see why.

One employee placed an X in Needs Improvement next to patient confidentiality, a federal mandate which the staff had to abide by, and put the following statement in the comment section:

As we walked through the waiting room, which was quite full, we could hear parts of the conversation at the registration desk. I even caught the individual's last name, and when the staff person repeated his Social Security number to make sure it was correct, everyone in the waiting room had to hear it. I know I did.

Duncan got out his red pen and placed a big X on the front of the Abby audit, knowing that this was a situation he would need to address first thing in the morning. They had discussed moving registration into an inner office, leaving a reception desk visible and manned for incoming patients, but it had never happened. Space constraints were always a concern in a growing hospital. However, it looked like now the situation couldn't be delayed any longer. They had to find an alternate place to admit incoming patients. He made a note to send Phillip and the head of the ER department an email about this first thing in the morning.

Another audit mentioned that the women's restroom needed attention—the wastebaskets were full—not unusual for late afternoon, but Duncan would look into it. Yet another thought the cafeteria needed a wider variety of vegan choices, something which Duncan thought had merit. Not an emergency by any means, but

he'd address it the next time he ran into Susan, who ran the facilities. A handful of audits addressed minor issues, like long waits for elevators. These were things that happened at a facility from time to time, depending on the time of day and the unpredictable circumstances they dealt with. But there was one that wasn't so common, and when Duncan saw it, he immediately picked up the phone.

Preventative Measures

The phone rang four times before Duncan heard the familiar friendly hello.

"Walker, Duncan here. Did I catch you at a bad time?"

"No, not at all. Just pouring a cup of coffee and getting ready to read the paper. What's up?"

"Well, you know we had a new group in for orientation today, right?"

"Sure, sure. I opened the door for most of them. Why?"

"Well, I had them do a tour of the hospital, telling them to walk around and do their own Abby audit."

"Smart move," Walker laughed, "getting the new guys to do your job for you."

"Hey, now give me some credit," Duncan joked. "But seriously, we have an issue here that I need to bring to your attention. I think you're gonna have to alert Security right away."

"Yes, sir," Walker replied, changing his tone to one of concern. "What's wrong?"

"Well, it seems that the group toured all of the usual areas, they walked through the ER, the cafeteria, and the hallways housing the patients' rooms. You know what I mean, the waiting rooms, and outpatient departments, the usual."

"Yeah…"

"Well, one of the audits indicated that they were able to get in to the nursery during non-visiting hours."

"Hmmm, wonder who buzzed them in," said Walker.

"That's just it, Chief," Duncan explained. "Nobody did. The door wasn't locked. They walked right in and weren't stopped. We could have a potentially major problem here, and I thought I'd let you know right away."

"You bet we could. I'm on it. I'll give my guys a call right away.

It looks like I need to make a quick trip to the hospital, just in case."

"Thanks, Walker. You know I wouldn't bother you at home if it wasn't important."

"I'm glad you did, Duncan. This is a breach that we can't afford to let happen. Meet up with me in the morning and I'll give you a report."

They said a quick goodbye, and Duncan turned his attention back to the rest of the audits, which, thankfully, didn't contain anything noteworthy. He felt a sense of relief, glad he'd brought home the folder, and even more happy that one very alert person had reported a potential problem that could have created traumatic results. The safety and security of newborn babies was something they took very seriously at Reliance, and that was one thing that could never be undermined. It was instances like these when Abby's true worth was exposed. Right now, the piece of paper in his hand was priceless.

No Room for Error

The commute to work the next morning was laborious. Rain pelted down on the highway, with occasional waves that were so heavy, the windshield wipers of his F-150 couldn't quite keep up. The truck was almost nine years old, but he'd taken good care of it and couldn't complain. Chosen specifically for its durability, it was the four-wheel drive capabilities that had earned Duncan's loyalty. Iowa winters were known to produce treacherous snowstorms, and there had been many blustery January days when he was glad he'd made the investment. With over 160,000 miles on it, Duncan knew he'd have to cave in and trade it for a newer model, but for now, he was certain he could nurse it along for another year. But he'd been looking at the new models, and he liked what he saw. When the time came, he'd get another F-150. When he found a brand that he liked and delivered what it promised, he stuck with it—now, if it only could make the rain go away.

The drive took 15 minutes longer than usual, and when Duncan pulled in, he spotted Walker's truck in the parking place designated Security. The umbrella over his head didn't offer total protection, so he and a few others sprinted toward the doors, where Walker was notably absent from his usual morning ritual of opening doors and keeping a watchful eye on the incoming and outgoing traffic and visitors. *Well, I guess I'll just have to catch up with him when I get upstairs*, Duncan thought.

After holding the door for an elderly woman who had been dropped off at the main entrance, Duncan folded his umbrella and entered the hospital. He was so busy shaking off the rain that he failed to notice Walker standing just off to the side, a good vantage point where he could still maintain his morning vigil.

"There you are," Walker said as he approached Duncan. "I've been waiting for you."

"Yeah, well, it's a gully washer out there, let me tell you. It's nothing short of luck that I'm only 15 minutes late."

"I'll agree with that. If you've got a sec, can you take a little walk with me?"

"Sure," Duncan replied, pulling off his overcoat as the two turned toward the west wing.

"Well, I called my men last night and had them check the lock on the obstetrics door, and then I called Maintenance to make sure they were on the up and up. By the time I got here, the situation was in control. Seems that the automatic lock had malfunctioned, so Maintenance immediately went to work to replace it, and I kept someone on guard until it was replaced and fully functional. We need to determine, though, how long it had been out of commission.

Something like this should not have gone unnoticed for any period of time. You have any suggestions on how we can do that?"

"Have you talked to the supervising RN?" asked Duncan.

"No, she came on at eight. Thought I'd give her a chance to complete the shift change, but her staff should have left her a report about it."

Using their key, they entered the floor and walked directly to the nurse's station.

"Hello, Duncan, Walker. What can I do for you?" said Mary Anne, the friendly, but no-nonsense, supervisor, as she looked up from the papers stacked on her desk.

Walker relayed the events of the previous night, asking her if she had been aware of whether the lock was or was not working the previous day. After she verified that she knew firsthand that it was working at some point earlier in the day, they assessed that the risk involved had been minimal. Once again, Duncan was grateful to whoever had shared the information.

"Well, I'm certainly happy that the situation was resolved. It would have been chaos in here today if people were walking in and out. We've got three new admissions about ready to deliver. I know why you're here, Walker, but Duncan? Let me guess, Abby again?"

"Yes, it seems that a new group doing the orientation tour caught it and was insightful enough to document it. I'm just glad I took their audits home with me last night. Otherwise, the situation could have ended quite differently. Maybe, Mary Anne, we should look into a backup system for those busy times or when you're not here to make sure everything is buttoned up."

"You're probably right. I'll take it up with Maintenance and see what they suggest. In the meantime, I'll direct my staff to make routine checks to ensure the floor is secure."

"Of course, Security will also bump up their rounds, as

well," added Walker.

"Good enough," Duncan replied. "If that's all, Walker, I need to get upstairs and put this wet stuff away."

"All right. Mary Anne, I'll see you later. Before you go, Duncan, are we still on for this afternoon?"

Pausing, Duncan momentarily forgot that his secretary had set up a meeting with Walker for 2:00 to discuss coordination of the traffic and communication of emergency personnel during the upcoming disaster drill. He'd better get to work; he had a lot of notes and potential problems that he wanted to iron out before the drill, and he had wanted Walker and his crew to be apprised of them at the meeting. The drill would illuminate several situations they hadn't previously encountered. Being prepared was the first call to action.

"Right, Walker. You bring the coffee," Duncan answered before turning toward the Staff Only elevator which would take him to his office and a morning full of emails and reports.

Staying Informed

Phillip Dobbins read through his emails, noting nothing of significance, outside of a meeting cancellation and the notification of a possible Security breach in the Nursery. The staff had taken swift action once it was brought to their attention, and everything was back to normal, which was all he really needed to know. *They know their jobs, and for the most part, they all do them very well*, he thought. Problems didn't concern Phillip—he often thrived on them and the challenge of correcting them. That's why he had brought Duncan on board to implement BrandSlaughter—and this was just another instance where it had proved its worth. By hiring people who were committed to Reliance's brand, he trusted them to its care. They weren't letting him down.

Turning his attention to present matters, Dobbins tackled the agenda for the monthly meeting of the Board of Directors. Besides covering the usual issues, financial reports, and accreditation updates, Thursday's meeting would also include a presentation by Dr. Alexander Barrett. Well versed in robotic cardiac surgery, Barrett's attraction to the hospital was largely attributed to the growth he could bring to their young, but well-respected cardiac unit. They would be using Thursday's meeting to discuss the advantages of the surgery, as well as the disadvantages, and the particulars of procuring the medical equipment and intensive training that the staff would require to implement it. This issue was vital to Dobbins, who knew that the future of the hospital relied heavily on its ability to provide the safest, but most recent, medical procedures. It was Dobbins's job to make sure the hospital's equipment was state-of-the-art and that his staff excelled in using it. To that end, he spent a great deal of his time working on the future development of their programs, trusting their staff with the day-to-day operations.

Sending off a "Job well done. I appreciate the update," email to Duncan, with a carbon copy to Walker, Phillip opened his computer's PowerPoint program and began the process of laying out the bullet points for Barrett's presentation. Of the many things that needed to be included in the presentation, Dobbins knew that the Board would be interested in justifying the investment in equipment, as well as the expense of additional staff and training that go hand in hand with new procedures. It would be his job to make those points. Barrett's job would be to sell them on the surgical procedure, while providing them with its advantages and potential ramifications. Usually, the Board took great pride in their successes, but it was also true that they took their role as fiduciaries seriously and never jumped on board unless they were absolutely certain that the hospital could sustain any potential

damage which might result. Thankfully, that hadn't been an issue since Phillip had taken over the reins as CEO.

Pushing the intercom button, Phillip asked his assistant to summon Vivian Daly and request the most recent figures for adding an additional cardiac surgeon, as well as hiring and training three additional RNs for the unit. By adding this new procedure, they were likely to attract patients from a wider geographic location. More patients merited more staff. Even if it was a safeguard, he wanted to provide the Board with complete disclosure on how the procedure would impact their needs. Yet, he didn't feel entirely comfortable with the presentation he'd pulled together yet...on paper, everything looked just fine. But, as it was with everything, it wasn't just what you knew that could cause bumps down the road. It was the things you didn't know—ignorance isn't always bliss. Chewing on his bottom lip, he stared at the monitor, trying to figure out just what was missing from the presentation, besides Dr. Barrett's expertise. Suddenly, a light bulb went off in his head and he reached for the phone.

"Duncan, Phil here. Can you come into my office for a few minutes? I want to brainstorm an idea with you."

Trial Runs

Ten minutes later, Duncan sat in the leather chair across from Phillip's desk and asked, "Whatcha got?"

"Well, Duncan, I'm working on a proposal to present to the Board for the purchase of the robotic surgical machine that will take us to the next level in cardiac surgery. I've got the advantages and benefits; that was easy. But now, I have to delicately word the potential disadvantages to the hospital for offering this surgery and how it could hypothetically harm us. But I want to do it in a positive light, meaning that I want to address potential problems, and then provide solutions or ways we will attempt to avoid them. It occurred to me that finding the negative aspects could be done in the same manner as an ABI audit. Can ABI be implemented in a hypothetical situation, one where we find potential, not existing, problems and proactively suggest a solution?"

"Sure, it can," replied Duncan. "In fact, it can be used to determine the merit or worth of an idea or a policy, as well as determining the outcome of one that's already in place. Let me give you an example. Do you remember how I used the story of Bubba and his tender ribs in orientations—you know, where I tell how Bubba had a disastrous grand opening, but how he could have prevented it if he'd done a trial run, anticipating every and any problem which might have arose, and then trained his staff to respond to each of those?"

"Yes, we all know about Bubba," Phillip sighed, waiting for Duncan to get to his point.

"Well, I suggest that you do a 'trial run' in this instance, too. Imagine that you have the equipment and the staff is already trained. What potential problems might you see? Maybe the expense doesn't justify the return, or maybe it's such a delicate surgery that there is a high likelihood of human error or equipment malfunction. Maybe the investment for training our staff in the equipment and the procedures is too high. Then again, what are the risks? Is it perfected yet, and how many people will actually benefit from the surgery?"

"All of those are things that I thought of, Duncan, but when you put them on paper, it begins to sound far too negative and risky. But I know that given time and training, this procedure has the potential to put us on the map nationally as a leader in minimally-invasive cardiac surgery. I'm so convinced of it that I went out on a limb

to recruit Dr. Barrett—one of the country's most respected and leading doctors in the field."

"Well, then I suggest that you write every one of those things down, pretend that they do happen, and then do what you do best, Phil—find the fastest, easiest, and most effective way to prevent them or correct them, should they come to fruition. But let me remind you that you will fail if you simply address the surgery and the equipment without tying it in with our brand. Remember, every hospital in the nation might someday have this equipment and offer this surgery. What does Reliance have that they don't? What is our God Only Knows factor that will make them select Reliance for this particular surgery? Is it just our geographic location and proximity to the patient? Put your finger on that, and you can overcome any and every objection the Board makes."

"Right now, Duncan, we have two things: our reputation for excellence and the fact that we have an esteemed expert in the field on our staff, Dr. Barrett."

"Well then, it looks like our Dr. Barrett is about to get a crash course in an Abby audit. Let's hope he's more receptive to it than he was at the orientation."

Potential Disaster

As Duncan had feared, his wife was developing an unfavorable opinion of her unit's new chief. That night, over grilled salmon and steamed vegetables, she vented.

"It's not that he's not capable or that he isn't talented, Duncan. He most certainly is. But, he's very short with the staff and some of them are walking on eggshells for fear that they'll be the recipient of his sharp tongue. More than that, though, I'm afraid he's not being compassionate enough with our patients. Their conversations are like 'yes, no, yes, no'—there isn't room for discussion. And when he walks out of the room, it's the nurses who are left explaining procedures and answering questions," Lynne said. "You should have seen the poor lab tech that he cornered today because some blood work he wanted wasn't done fast enough. She was a nervous wreck."

"Hmmm. Isn't he working under Slater still?" Duncan asked, referring to the outgoing chief who was retiring at the end of the month.

"Sure, he is. But they don't seem to be working together. It's more like Slater's showing him the ropes when he needs to know a specific thing, but other than that, they stay out of each other's way."

"Too bad we can't mix Slater and Barrett together and come up with someone who has the best of both—Barrett's success in the O.R., and Slater's bedside manner," replied Duncan.

"That would probably be too much to ask," Lynne

retorted.

Is it? Duncan wondered. Isn't this exact situation the reason the mentor program was developed and implemented at the hospital? Why was it, though, that it worked so well with the nurses and all of the other employees, but when it came to chiefs of staff, nobody wanted to say anything or step on their toes?

Duncan had witnessed Barrett's demeanor in the afternoon meeting with Phil that day, and he had the same worries that his wife had voiced. Barrett knew he was good and gave the impression that he didn't have to be bothered with such insignificant matters as developing rapport with the other employees or the patients. Experience had proven that such an attitude wouldn't go over well when attempting to win the Board's approval for major purchases and renovations to their cardiac surgical unit.

On paper, he knew it would look good—Phillip would make sure of that. But winning the approval of the people whose job was to protect the hospital and its financial outlook would require some finesse—something Barrett was apparently lacking. *How can we get Barrett to tap into Slater's demeanor*, he asked himself, *What's it going to take to bring him around and make him a good fit?*"

As Duncan pondered that question, his mind went back to the meeting and Barrett's response to the fact that they were going to do a crash BrandSlaughter audit on the ramifications of the hospital acquiring the new equipment and implementing the medical procedure. As Phillip explained to him the necessity of presenting both the advantages and disadvantages to the Board, the surgeon had vehemently disagreed, stating that under his watchful eye, there was no room for error. That was good to know, but as Phillip and Duncan's eyes met across the desk, they also knew that it was highly unlikely. Along with changes come challenges, and walking in with blinders on, refusing to accept that there might, and most likely would, be unforeseeable problems was a recipe for disaster.

Speaking of disaster, Duncan reminded himself, *I nearly forgot about the upcoming disaster drill. I still have to develop an audit for it, and I've only got a little more than a week to do it.* As he finished the food on his plate, he sighed, thinking that he just might have piled too much on his plate. It was going to be another long night, he thought, as he put his plate in the sink and grabbed his briefcase.

Probing Questions

Phillip hustled into the boardroom and exchanged greetings with the members who were already seated around the dark

cherry conference table. One glance at the equipment at the front of the room told him that his assistant had already booted the computer and loaded his presentation. All he had to do was click the mouse when they were ready to begin.

Alexander Barrett walked in a few minutes later. Since the meeting hadn't started, Phillip took the opportunity to personally introduce their new hire to the Board members, hoping that the more casual introduction would break the ice and warm him up, if only a little.

After covering the regular agenda items, including approval and acceptance of expenditures and the monthly financial report, they rolled into the meeting. First, he informed the Board of the disaster drill, slated to occur a week from Saturday. The Board members listened intently and commended the practice run, stating that it would be a good opportunity to see if they could handle a calamity of major proportions.

"I'd certainly be interested in receiving a follow-up report with the results, Phillip," said the hospital's attorney.

"Of course," replied Phillip. "In fact, Duncan Edwards, our in- house auditor, will be conducting an Abby audit during the drill. He'll be working closely with Security and Gina, our spokesperson, to minimize the additional traffic inside and outside the hospital, as well as the expected onslaught of media inquiries that we can expect during a community emergency. Walker's already busy devising a plan to keep the flow of traffic from bottlenecking so emergency vehicles can get in and out. These are just a few of the unique challenges we hope to address before there is a real need. It will be a learning process, indeed. I'll make sure you all get copies of Duncan's audit when it's completed, and we'll discuss it at the next Board meeting."

"In fact, Duncan, Dr. Barrett and I have completed an audit for the next proposal on the agenda. Dr. Barrett comes to Reliance with impressive credentials. As you all know, Reliance has been diligently concentrating its efforts on its cardiac surgery unit, and we've quickly attained five-star status with our success rate and patient satisfaction. It is our hope that we can become one of the top 100 hospitals in the nation for cardiac surgery, and with Dr. Barrett's expertise and experience, I believe that can be achieved. To that end, we are proposing the addition of one of the newer technological procedure sin cardiac surgery, using robotic surgery that is less invasive, which allows patients to heal faster and shortens their hospital stay. This reduces several risks common among heart surgery patients, like infection and blood clots. Without further ado, I'll turn the floor over to Dr. Barrett, so he can introduce you to the equipment and the procedure."

Dr. Barrett rose and stepped to the front of the room, turning his head to the monitor on the wall. As he flipped from one slide to another, he described the robotic surgical machine in detail, including its dimensions and specifications. Phillip was again reminded why he was impressed with Barrett's credentials—the man certainly knew what he was talking about. He seemed to have an encyclopedic memory and knowledge of the equipment and the procedure as he touted its benefits to the hospital and to its patients.

"Are there any questions?" Barrett asked when he completed his recitation.

"Yes, I'd like to know what the success rate is for the procedure and what the risks are," spoke their attorney.

"Well, let's take those questions one at a time. The success rate among those who are trained and certified in performing the surgery is comparable to, and often better than, open heart surgery. It depends on many factors, including the age, health, and overall condition of the patient. The risks are few and usually are avoidable," Barrett answered.

"But what are those risks?" prodded the lawyer.

This is precisely why we needed to audit this before presenting it, thought Phillip. The Board will thoroughly consider the risks, and Barrett doesn't seem to want to entertain them in the discussion.

"Of course there are risks," interjected Phillip. "Just as in any health or surgical procedure, there will be risks. There is a risk of infection, and we will minimize that risk by imposing the same stringent standards of sterilization that we stress throughout the hospital. One of the other risks worthy of consideration is the possibility of error, mechanical or human. To minimize those possibilities, staff will be trained in the inspection and maintenance of the robot, which will be performed before and after each use. In addition, all surgeons, nurses, assistants and anesthesiologists who will be involved in these surgeries will be required to attend training and receive certification, which will be done in-house, and they will have to observe a specific number of surgical procedures which utilize the equipment before they are allowed to be a member of the operating team."

"Phillip, I'm going to turn the conversation to a loaded question," said Gary, their accountant. "Just how much does this equipment cost and what are the financial estimates for such extensive and technical training? Do you have the numbers?"

"Yes, I do. In your folders, you'll find a cost estimate for the acquisition of the equipment, the special space requirements which must be dedicated to it, and the extensive training necessary. Yes, it's a significant amount—but we believe that the returns it will bring to Reliance and the health and welfare of our patients justify that expense. If approved, Dr. Barrett and I will travel to New York later in the month and speak directly to the manufacturer, and I'll get a personal demonstration and opportunity to see the procedure being implemented. Anyone who is interested is welcome to join us."

"Well, I can certainly see the advantage this brings to our patients and the community, but do you know of any areas where it could be perceived negatively to our image?" asked the Board's public relations manager.

"I've thought about this considerably, and Duncan and I

have poured over several possibilities. First, we want the public to approve of the procedure, but we don't want to overdo it and give the impression that it's a miracle machine. It's not. So our publicity efforts and the way we inform the community will have to be in a positive light, but will also have to include disclaimers, informing them about possible risk factors. It will be a balancing act. Second, assuming the fact that this offering receives community support, we'll also have to deal with patients who demand robotic surgery over its counterpart, but who, for various reasons, might not be good candidates for it. This will require open doctor-patient communication, with thorough explanations and thoughtful considerations for the patients' needs and wants, as well as the outcome and success of their surgical options. Because Reliance strives at all times to be a hospital that stresses a caring environment, this will be one of our highest priorities," Phillip explained, as he turned his head and spoke the last words directly to Dr. Barrett.

Practice Makes Perfect

Walker's thumb hit the walkie talkie button, alerting his entire staff to switch channels. Then, he verified that everyone was in the proper places and ready.

From his station near the main entrance, Walker had a good view—he could see the officer directing traffic in front of the now disengaged traffic light at the hospital entrance. This would allow them to move emergency vehicles through without any delays. He could also see the emergency room entrance, the main parking lot, and the reception area just 20 feet inside the main doors. Not only was he overseeing security and traffic flow today, but he would also be assisting and directing people entering the hospital, much like he did every morning.

The mock drill was a big test for Walker's security department—truth be told, Reliance was a mid-size hospital, and the town had a low-crime rate. The traffic in and out of the institution was even and consistent. Outside of a fender bender or the rare occasion when someone backed into another car in the parking lot, traffic control wasn't an issue. As he zipped up his light jacket against the chill of the morning air, Walker longed for a cup of hot coffee, but he knew that in just a few minutes, coffee would be the last thing on his mind.

Turning his head to the glass doors behind him, he could see that the Reception Desk was prepared. Lois, their full-time receptionist, had been joined by Samantha, one of their new hires who took the weekend and a couple evening shifts each week. She'd proven to be a quick study, but even so, Walker knew that today could be a receptionist's nightmare. Just as in a real disaster, phone calls were scheduled to be made to mimic the increased activity and inquiries, and the media and volunteers who were participating in the event would be directed to the front desk, where they would receive assistance.

Sticking his head inside the doors, Walker asked the ladies if they'd heard from Gina.

"Yes, Mr. Briggs," confirmed Samantha. "She's in the conference room—she said the cooks and servers were already bringing in a stream of coffee and donuts for the morning rush, so if you're looking for your morning coffee, now's the time."

"No thanks, Sam, but I do appreciate the offer. Just checking to make sure I can start sending people her way when they arrive."

And it was a good thing he turned down the offer, because it wasn't 30 seconds later that Walker heard the first siren. He pulled the walkie talkie to his face, pushed the button, and said, "We're on."

From that moment, the day was a hustle of activity. The first two or three emergency vehicles came and went without a hitch, transporting victims from the mock tornado which had blown the roof of the gym at the high school, leaving many students and teachers injured or missing. But then, as in all events, drills or otherwise, onlookers or gapers as they are sometimes called, followed the action, wanting to know what was going on. Although it had been announced by the press that today's drill was not a real disaster, it was obvious that it had attracted those who were curious or didn't get the newspaper. It wasn't long before lights and sirens were backed up, waiting down the road to get through the congestion.

"Good thing this is only practice, huh?"

Walker turned to find Duncan standing by his side, clipboard in hand.

"Yeah—I've called for an additional officer for traffic control. It's obvious that we need to intervene at the main road, instead of waiting until traffic gets within a couple blocks. Hopefully, that will steer some of the cars away and give us some space to get the emergency vehicles through."

"You know, this reminds me of a concert I once attended," Duncan said. "It was back home—as I recall, it was put on to raise funds for charity. Anyway, the main group was a big name—with lots of number one hits. Everybody, and I mean everybody, got tickets for the show. This was a big deal for our town. The doors opened an hour before the concert, and when I got there, the line was already backed up. I'd guess it was at least a block and a half long. For some reason, they weren't prepared, and they only had two people scanning tickets and admitting the audience. I'm not kidding ya, it had to have been about 100 degrees that night and people were miserable and cranky. To make a long story short, some people didn't get in the doors until half an hour after the concert was supposed to start. By the time they got in, they were sold out of cold drinks, too. So, before the concert even began, most of the people were not happy campers. The concert was good when it finally started, but the lack of planning left a bad impression with a lot of people. It was the last time they attempted a concert—which was too bad. If they'd planned for the things that might have gone wrong, it would have been a real big success. As it was, they promised everyone a great time, but they didn't deliver. They simply weren't prepared to handle the crowd."

"Back to the old external branding stories, are you, Duncan? Don't worry—I get it. We're responding just as fast as we can. Look, it's already clearing out a little," he said, nodding toward the road where a van from the local television station was pulling in to the parking lot, followed by a squad car.

"Oh great…the news. Wonder how long it took them to get through. Well, you've got it under control, Walker. Well done. If you need anything, I'm here—oh, and make sure the reporter doesn't get in anyone's way. Send the news crew to the conference room. Gina's ready."

The first face Duncan saw in the auditorium was Phillip's. Swerving left and right to avoid the growing crowd, he made his way to his side.

"How is everything going, Phil? Any problems here?"

"It looks like Gail has everything under control. She just asked the servers to bring in more coffee—it's going fast. But, other than that, we only seem to have one problem with the number of requests that we might have in a disaster situation. There doesn't appear to be any real, credible means of updating our information. When parents come in seeking information about their youngsters, we want to be able to tell them if they are here, where they are at, and where they can find out about their condition. I've noticed there seems to be a lag from the time the victim is brought in until our records here are updated. We'll have to work on that. I mean, can you imagine the chaos and the frustration if this was real? We'd probably have somepretty angry and demanding parents on our hands, and to tell you the truth, I wouldn't blame them."

"Hmm, that's interesting. We'll have to have someone work on that—maybe through IT, where our computer records are updated instantly and accessible to all staff who are privileged to access it. Could be a challenge, but I can understand your concern. People expect us to be informed and to inform them on a timely basis. Tell me, Phil, have you witnessed this issue being addressed at any other hospitals? How did they handle it?"

"Well, usually it's not addressed until it has to be, which will be one good outcome of this drill. But, I can tell you that a lack of preparedness for scenarios such as this can be a publicity nightmare, and that's one thing I want to avoid at all costs, if possible."

"You're telling me. All of our promotional materials claim that we can be trusted to provide fast medical care in a caring environment. I can just see the headlines: 'Trust Reliance to Provide Care, Lose Patients.' Ouch.

"Don't go there, Duncan. Don't go there," Phil said, shaking his head as he walked away. Duncan returned to the emergency room entrance, observing quietly, while the doctors and nurses hustled from one room to another, tending to their patients. He was impressed with the way they took time with each one, as if they were really injured. Even the nurses who were giving going-home instructions to kids with fake sutures, crutches, and slings didn't miss a step. From all appearances, they were working as a team, which was something he gladly noted on his chart.

The automatic doors to the ER entrance opened, and Duncan looked down the hall, seeing a mother struggling to hold up her daughter, who appeared to about 12 or 13. Realizing she needed help, he put down his clipboard, but before he got there, a custodian already had grabbed a wheelchair and had taken the young girl's arm in his hand. As Duncan watched, the girl was lowered in the chair, much to her mother's relief, and the custodian personally volunteered to wheel her into triage and help her mother find immediate assistance. Within 30 seconds, the mother was relaying her daughter's symptoms to an RN—high fever, lethargic, intense stomach pains. In the midst of the commotion of the drill, Duncan observed the girl being wheeled into a room and heard their resident pediatrician being paged.

That's what it's all about, Duncan thought. *Helping people, even when your resources are stretched.* He quickly made a notation on the side of his paper, reminding himself to commend the young custodian who assisted the mother and let his supervisor know about his deed.

It's people like him who make us proud. Kudos to him and his concern for the well-being of our patients and their families. It's acts like these that precisely represent our brand and confirms that Reliance lives up to its

The Calm Before the Storm

Phillip's head was spinning, hoping he hadn't forgotten anything. The last three weeks had been busy. First was the Board meeting and getting the approval for the acquisition of the robotic surgical equipment, which, thankfully, went through without any significant opposition. Then, they held the mock drill on a much larger scale than ever before attempted. With a few exceptions, everything had gone smoothly, although Phillip was the first to admit that there were improvements that could be made, as evidenced by the Brand Integrity Audit Duncan had laid on his desk several days after the drill.

As usual, even amidst heavier than normal traffic in and out of their facility, the cleanliness and appearance of the hospital had earned top ratings. The staff, too, had completed their tasks efficiently and given their time constraints, with as much compassion and individual attention as possible. He was particularly impressed with the observation that a custodian provided assistance to a young girl who had been brought in with appendicitis and had asked Duncan to send the employee their esteemed F award for exemplifying qualities that made him a good fit. Appreciating and recognizing employees for a job well done was one area he firmly believed in.

However, the audit did reveal a few minor areas where improvement was needed. The initial congestion of traffic was one, but Walker had addressed it, immediately rectifying the problem. At one point, the receptionists stated they were backed up, both with requests for information and directions from people who were part of the drill and others who were conducting regular hospital business and visits. But, they quickly tended to every one of them, and admitted that no one had to wait for an extended period of time for assistance.

One of the major issues that Phillip knew he had to address right away was the inability to effectively obtain patient information from the emergency room. The hospital's computer system held information for every patient admitted into the hospital, but since the majority of the patients were treated in the emergency room, their information was not accessible. Usually, people were not formally input into the central database, which was available at all computers within the hospital, until they had been admitted and assigned a room. The mock disaster drill made him aware that changes needed to be made to their system, so together with IT, Phillip called for an upgrade to their software programs. He had just received word yesterday that the upgrades were completed, and now anyone who logged in to the central database could obtain information on anyone being treated at the hospital, even on an outpatient basis.

Snapping his suitcase shut, he grabbed his briefcase and walked into the kitchen to have a quick cup of coffee with Jill before he left. As he walked past his son, who was eating a bowl of Cheerios, he rubbed his head. "How's it going there, sleepyhead?" he asked, getting only a groan in return.

"Where's Sara?" he asked his wife.

"In her room, as usual. You know how long it takes a girl to change her clothes 20 times. She'll be out soon, crying because she has 'absolutely nothing to wear'."

"I'll give her a ride to school. Maybe then you won't have to hear it for so long."

"Thanks, I'd appreciate that. Are you packed and ready to go?"

"Yeah. I'm going to go into the office for an hour or so before I have to catch my flight. But first, I thought I'd check and see if there is a piece of that pie left. I'm starving."

Blueberry had been the flavor of the week, and Phillip admitted he'd had more than his fair share of the pie. But, he also had to admit that his weekly pies from Blues were one of the few indulgences he allowed himself. He really didn't know what it was about that place— sure the pie was good, but the atmosphere was nothing to write home about. What he did know, though, was that he looked forward to walking into the café every week and saying hi to the waitress and the owners, who all knew him by name. Even if I found a better-tasting pie somewhere else, Phillip admitted to himself, I'd still give them my business. It must be that God Only Knows factor, because I'm a customer for life.

"I was ready for that," Jill said, as she placed his pie and a cup of coffee on the table. "So, tell me, are you excited about this trip? Are any of the members of the Board going, too?"

"No, just me and Dr. Barrett," Phillip answered. "That might be a good thing, though. Some one-on-one time might do us some good. I'd like to get to know him a little better, and so far, that hasn't happened. As a matter of fact, nobody seems to have been able to get close to him. He's a great surgeon, but personality-wise, nobody can form an opinion one way or another, except to say that there has been a little improvement in his bedside manner since we specifically requested that he shadow Dr. Slater as he makes his rounds. He seems to have caught on a bit, and at least under his presence, is making an effort to connect with the patients and our staff. Let's just hope it sticks."

"That's good to hear," Jill said. "Let's also hope you don't get stuck in New York. They are calling for the possibility of an early snow or ice storm."

"Don't worry—I'll be fine. It's just a quick trip to the Big Apple. We'll check out the robot and meet with the manufacturer, get our order placed, and I'll be home before you know it. You probably won't even know I'm gone."

"Well, the one thing I do know is that you'll be home before Monday," she said, leaning across to pick up his empty plate. "I know you won't miss a week without your pie," she teased.

"Very funny, hon. You just hold the fort down here, but stay away from my pie," Phillip said, then gave his wife a kiss, rubbed his son's head again, and yelled, "Sara! Come on! You're going to be late for school!"

Growing Pains

Phillip left a few last-minute instructions with his assistant before grabbing his overcoat off the hook and rushing to catch the limo. As usual, Walker popped out of nowhere and held the door open for him.

"You have a good trip, Mr. Dobbins. And don't worry about a thing—I'll keep an eye on things here."

"I know you will, Walker. Thank you," Phillip replied as he walked through the double doors. "If you need anything, I've got my cell, and I've told Duncan to be on standby, just in case."

"That's good to know, but don't worry—we can get along without you for a few days."

"Somehow, Walker, I think that was supposed to make me feel good," Phillip laughed. "Oh, have you seen Barrett yet? Our driver should be waiting."

"Yes, sir. Your driver arrived ten minutes ago," he said, pointing to the dark blue sedan parked in the patient pick-up area. "Dr. Barrett's already in the car."

"Very well. I'll see you in a few days, Walker," Phillip said as he pulled his overcoat around his waist, guarding against the cold rain that had just started falling. Looking up, the sky was gray and gloomy—one of those skies that didn't show any promise of sunshine any time soon, he thought.

The driver opened the door before he got to the car and placed his suitcase in the trunk while Phillip settled into the plush leather seat next to Dr. Barrett, who was intently reading what looked to be a medical periodical. "Good morning," Phillip said, nodding toward the surgeon.

"Oh, good. You're here. Now we can finally be on our way," said Dr. Barrett.

The driver back behind the wheel, they pulled out and started their trek to the airport. Phillip took the opportunity to settle in and get comfortable. For a brief moment, he thought about pulling out his briefcase and tackling some paperwork, but dismissed that notion in favor of making small talk with the surgeon seated next to him. This was, after all, a good opportunity for them to get to know one another better.

"So, I trust that everything's under control while you'll be gone. Any particular issues or concerns that I can help with?" Phillip opened.

"No, Dr. Slater is still there, and as you know, he's quite capable. Though, I do believe he's rather slow—we could tend to more patients if there was less chit chat."

"Well, I do understand what you're saying, doctor. But, Dr. Slater is well known for the relationships he's established with the patients at Reliance. It's been a benefit, in my opinion, not a deterrent, to the department. Can I ask what you would change, given the opportunity?"

"I'd push more patients through. Doctors, especially surgeons, don't need to know all the details of a patient's life—just the ones that are necessary to make a proper diagnosis and prescribe the best treatment," Barrett answered, slowly becoming more involved in the conversation.

"I respectfully disagree, doctor. You see, my position is different than yours—in my role, I have to take into account the overall perception of the hospital—not just one particular department. I find that the community is best served when we connect with them, even if that means patient by patient. I also find that the best way for us to provide quality services isn't by pushing patients through in a faster timeframe, but rather by working together as a team. That's the most effective way to accomplish more in less time."

"That may work in other areas, but my focus is on cardiac surgery. I don't have time to worry about what everyone else in the hospital is doing."

"I agree, in part, and heartily admit that the cardiac surgery is a vital part of our hospital and the services we provide. That's one reason we're making this trip today. But, there is still something to be said for community outreach and enhancing the public's perception of the care they receive at Reliance," Phillip replied. Rubbing his chin, he contemplated a better way of describing his vision to the doctor.

"Look at it this way. Let's say that you are a customer of a bank, let's call it The People's Bank. A few blocks away sits another bank, which we'll call Bank-In-a-Minute. Now, at The People's Bank, everybody knows you. You've been banking there for years. They call you by name, and you know their employees by name. When you walk up to a teller, she asks how you're doing and asks about your family. Sometimes, they punch up your accounts before you even start your transaction. And when it comes time to apply for a loan, it's a pleasant experience—your personal banker knows you, your reputation and your finances. Can you see the benefits of banking there?"

"Sure."

"Over at Bank-In-a-Minute, most transactions are conducted through the drive-through windows—you know, those tinted windows where you can't really see the tellers very well. They base their progress on how many customers they can serve in a day. They don't have any interest in getting to know you—they're a numbers bank. And when it comes time to get a loan, you have to walk inside and deal with a stranger. To them, you're a piece of paper. Pretty cold and impersonal, right?"

"Maybe, but efficient, I might add."

"Yes, it is efficient. But when both banks offer the same incentives, interest, and services, which one do you think will attract the most customer loyalty? Which one will leave a positive and lasting impression upon the customer—one that makes him want to do business with them and want to come back again?"

"I get where you're going with this. Yes, some level of interaction is necessary, but keep in mind, though, that it can be in excess, which is not productive," Barrett interjected.

"There is a fine line between the two, doctor. My job is to make sure that we maintain an even balance. If we didn't, I'd be committing BrandSlaughter."

"That term again," Dr. Barrett mused. "BrandSlaughter, a funny name for a hospital policy. Let me ask, what's the point?"

"Ahhh, I'm glad you asked. You see, I once asked myself the very same thing—that is, until I met Duncan at a seminar about ten years ago. He opened my eyes to the BrandSlaughter concept, which by the way, isn't a policy. It's an audit, or a way of measuring our adherence to our brand, as well as our progress and growth."

"Continue."

"Okay, I will. Now, Alex—may I call you Alex?" "I suppose."

"Good. Now, let me ask, what happens to the heart when it's neglected—when a patient doesn't exercise, eats fatty foods that are high in cholesterol, and fails to monitor their blood pressure?"

"Well, most of the time, we'll see weight gain, clogged arteries, and an increase in bad cholesterol in the blood. The heart, which is a muscle, has to overexert itself to compensate for the extra weight, but it is forced to work even harder because it hasn't been strengthened by cardiovascular exercise. All of these put even further strain on the heart and the patient's overall health, and the health problems which result place even more undue stress on the heart. There are many other potential problems which could result…

"No, that's good enough. You see, our brand is much like a heart. Actually, it is at the heart of what we are all about. If we neglect the most important aspects of our brand, it is weakened, just as the heart is when it's neglected. Then, we have to work harder in everything we do to compensate for our weaknesses. Not only do we see additional stress among our staff and our patients, but one by one, other parts of the system start to weaken and break down. But when we're in brand integrity, it's like having a strong heart. So, I guess you could think of Abby—our Audit of Brand Integrity—as a complete physical, letting us know if we're healthy, but especially pointing out areas where our brand is weak, so we can work together to strengthen it again."

"Well, that certainly makes more sense to me than talking about ribs," replied Barrett.

"Maybe," chuckled Phillip. "But the point is, all parts of the body need the heart, and it's also true that the heart functions best when all parts of the body are working properly. At Reliance, Alex, all parts of the hospital need our brand, but it's also true that the brand is strongest when all areas of the hospital work together cohesively to maintain our brand's health."

"And your BrandSlaughter audit is like a stress test or a heart checkup?"

"Precisely," smiled Phillip. "I think you've got it."

Bringing Out the Best

The plane landed on time at the John F. Kennedy Airport. The flight was uneventful and for the two men, spent mostly in silence. Dr. Barrett was again engrossed in a medical journal, and Phillip used the time to address the most pressing items in his briefcase. After going through baggage claim, they maneuvered their way through the crowd and out the exit doors, where they took turns attempting to hail a cab.

"It's a good thing it's not raining like it was back in Iowa," Phillip remarked.

A few minutes later, they were seated in the backseat of a rundown taxi, on their way to check in at the hotel. "I'm glad I don't have to deal with this traffic and congestion every day," Phillip said. "Des Moines isn't anything compared to this."

Dr. Barrett simply looked at him, seemingly not affected by the bumper-to-bumper traffic. Phillip had to remind himself that not too long ago, this was Barrett's home, so he endured the rest of the cab ride in silence.

Their appointment at the university's medical center was scheduled for 3:15, just enough time for Phillip to stow away his bags and let Jill know they'd arrived safely. When she reported that the forecast for the next couple days called for a mixture of ice and rain, Phillip told her to stay in if it got messy. There was nowhere they had to be that was important enough to risk traveling on slick roads.

He met Dr. Barrett in the lobby and gladly let him take

charge as he directed the cab driver to the university's medical center. Upon their arrival, Dr. Barrett's familiarity with the institution allowed them to easily navigate the maze to the office of the Chief Cardiologist, who Barrett greeted enthusiastically. It was evident that the surgeon was at ease and had a respected and long-established relationship with his peer—the enthusiasm and friendliness he exhibited toward the chief were traits that Phillip had not yet witnessed. He found them to be both pleasant and promising.

Next came a tour of the facilities, one of the main attractions for Phillip during this visit. Based on their observations, he and Dr. Barrett would be instrumental in designing the space dedicated for the robotic equipment and surgery. Today's tour would serve as their basic blueprint.

When they entered the room which housed the robot, Dr. Barrett immediately crossed the gleaming tiled floor to inspect the robot, which was installed aside a steel surgical bed. From there, he pointed out the computer console from which the surgeon directed the robot's movements. Barrett was animated as he described the

procedure, and Phillip noticed himself catching the excitement. Indeed, the possibility of a surgeon performing bypass surgery without ever touching a patient was phenomenal.

There was something about Barrett that came alive when he described the robot and its functions. It was an energetic and contagious enthusiasm born from a passion for his specialty. *It's exactly that enthusiasm and energy that I want to bottle and take back with us to Iowa,* Phillip thought. *If the rest of the staff could see him now, they'd be impressed, too, I'm sure.*

Phillip closely watched as the two surgeons demonstrated the robot's capabilities, interjecting every few minutes for clarification or further information. With every inquiry, Dr. Barrett was patient and thorough in his response. *Now if I can just get him to exemplify those traits with our patients,* thought Phillip.

After the demonstration, the three went to lunch before their scheduled meeting with the manufacturer of the robot. That meeting gave Phillip access to the engineer who would provide them with the specs and requirements for its installation and operation. All in all, it was a productive and enlightening day.

When Emergencies Happen

Well, what did you think? Do you have any doubts about offering minimally invasive surgery at Reliance?" Dr. Barrett asked Phillip on the return flight home.

"Not at all—I'm cautious, but excited about the prospects and opportunities it will bring to us," replied Phillip. "However, the key is to remember that its reception to the public will be largely determined by how we market it. We have to be careful that we don't oversell it, leaving people with the impression that it's a cure-all and a wonder robot. Because if we do, at some point, they're bound to be disappointed when they learn that there are risks and that nothing is foolproof."

"Yes, I can see that, but how do we walk that fine line? After all, the technology is one of a kind and, in my opinion, long overdue. What more can we do than promote its benefits, while giving the standard disclaimer that all medical procedures entail risk?"

"Hmm, that's a good question, and one which I've been thinking about. My biggest concern is that we must address all factors, good and bad, when we offer patients with this surgery. The way we do that will certainly affect our brand."

"How so?" asked the doctor, seemingly interested in where the conversation was going.

"Well, maybe the best way to explain it is by using an example that is not related to medicine. How about a political campaign— better yet, a candidate for President of the United States?"

"Go ahead."

"Okay, so let's say a candidate ran for office, promising several key factors, like economic growth, no tax increases, and clean energy. When he traveled, the country delivering those promises, he built his brand. Those promises actually became his brand—they are what he stood for and represented. Now, let's say he is elected based on those promises. People bought his brand, right? But when he got into office, he didn't deliver. He didn't keep his promises to the voters who supported him. Now, they are disillusioned and discouraged as the economy takes a nose dive and the President does an about face, insisting that a tax increase is necessary to balance the budget. They're not buying this guy's brand anymore because it's not what he said it would be. The very same people who brought him success and voted him in will be the people who work to make sure he loses the next time. He lost their loyalty. So, doctor, in this situation, how do you think the promotion of the President's brand hurt his image and approval rating?"

"That's easy. He promised people the world, but didn't carry through with his promises—for whatever reasons. Now, the people don't believe they were being told the truth—they think they've been had."

"A-ha!, I think you've got it," Phillip said, smiling. "The same thing will apply to our promotion and marketing efforts. We have to be forthright and up front with the public and tell them all the pros and cons so they can make their own informed decisions. We can't make the decision for them by making grand claims that we can't support. It is the way that we give them the information they need to make their own decision that will affect our brand. That's where you will play a pivotal role in our success, Doctor. You're the guy running for office here and making promises. People will base their vote on your campaign. You have to give them full disclosure and answer all of their questions thoroughly and honestly. You have to be the representative of our brand and make sure that you don't over promise and under deliver."

"I'm a surgeon, not a PR agent," Dr. Barrett half-heartedly chuckled. "But I think I understand what you're saying. If we're going to make Reliance one of the top cardio-surgical hospitals in the Midwest, I better start shaking a lot of hands. But while I'm earning the approval of the patients, I have to be sensitive to their ability to make informed decisions based on promises I know I can deliver. Am I right, Phillip?" Dr. Barrett asked.

"Indeed, you are. But you're not alone—I'll be on the campaign trail with you the whole time. As a team, we'll work together to make sure that we can deliver the brand we promise and that those who place their trust in us don't have any reason to accuse us of BrandSlaughter."

Ladies and gentlemen, please place all cargo in the storage departments and buckle your seatbelts. We're encountering icy conditions as we near Des Moines International Airport. We will keep you updated on any further reports, announced the steward.

Ahhh, I forgot. Jill did mention that the forecast had been calling for sleet. For once, it looked like the forecasters got it right, Phillip thought. Meteorologists might just be the only occupation that can get away with promising one thing and delivering another. But Jill had found one she trusted—she swore by the forecasts made by Kate Kevins, her favorite local meteorologist—proof again that it doesn't matter what industry you're in, your brand is what builds your loyalty.

The passengers were notified that landing would be delayed while the grounds crew worked to de-ice the runway. When they were finally given clearance, the captain thanked the passengers for their patience and notified them that there would be a delay on the ground because they would not be able to taxi to the gate due to icy conditions. The flight attendants made their rounds, checking seat belts and securing overhead storage bins.

Prepared for a less than smooth landing, Phillip was not surprised when he looked out the window during their descent and saw that the runway was lined with emergency vehicles. Red and yellow fire trucks, ambulances, and foam trucks were ready to line up in pursuit of the aircraft upon landing. Understanding that this was protocol in the event of hazardous weather, Phillip wasn't concerned, but was instead reassured by the precautions taken.

The plane touched ground, braking and bouncing several times before the wheels grabbed hold of the runway underneath. As predicted, the emergency crews pulled out one by one, following the 747 as it rolled down the runway. Near the end of the runway, the plane hit a patch of ice and slid dangerously to the right, where an industrial steel fence separated the airport from an embankment and the expressway which ran adjacent to it. As the passengers braced themselves for potential impact, the pilot scraped the fence, not just once, but twice—the force jerking the secured passengers from one side to another. Suddenly, the pilot somehow regained footing and brought the plane to an abrupt, but very rough rest.

Ladies and gentlemen, please remain seated and in your seatbelts. Your flight attendants will be around shortly. If you need assistance, please notify them, announced the captain.

"Excuse me, doctor," the steward said to Dr. Barrett. "The captain would like to see you both."

Phillip and Dr. Barrett were escorted to the cockpit, where the captain asked the doctor to assist in administering emergency first aid for anyone who might have been injured. After agreeing, they began to assess their fellow passengers for potential injuries, while the flight attendants assured the passengers that everything was under control and that the airline was en route with a bus to transport them to their terminal.

Determining that there were passengers in need of further medical treatment—several had shoulder and arm pains and potential whiplash, another had hit his head and likely needed stitches and an X-ray to rule out a concussion or head injury, and an elderly woman with a history of high blood pressure was short of breath—Dr. Barrett addressed each passenger, while Phillip assisted him in dressing wounds and obtaining ice packs. All in all, given the potential for a much more serious accident, they had fared relatively well.

All passengers remained seated while emergency personnel loaded the accident victims for transportation to Reliance Hospital.

Dr. Barrett and Phillip were next, being allowed to accompany the victims to the hospital.

As they neared the hospital, Phillip noticed that officers were directing traffic, ensuring that the emergency vehicles didn't encounter any delays. Pulling into the emergency room entrance, Phillip was met by Walker.

"Are you okay, sir?"

"Fine, Walker, I'm fine. We've got a few incoming injuries, though, thankfully, most are not major."

"We're ready, sir. The airport notified us that we should be prepared for potential injuries before landing. We've called in staff and have implemented our emergency disaster plan."

"Very good, Walker. Our ER's going to be busy for a while, though, and I'm guessing that the phone lines might encounter higher than usual traffic, but I don't believe that it's anything that we can't handle. Do you have an update on the weather forecast? The last thing we need is an onslaught of traffic accidents right now."

"Yes, sir. I've been in touch with the state police and am getting reports from the National Weather Service. Looks like we've got a few more hours before this front pulls through."

"Thanks, Walker. Keep me posted if you can. I'd better check and see how Duncan's doing," Phillip said, turning toward the emergency room. "Good job, Walker. Keep it up."

"Thank you. Oh, and sir—it's good to have you back."
"It's good to be back, Walker. Thank you."

At Ease

Phillip found Duncan at the emergency room registration desk, validating that the new outpatient software program was operating as expected—it was certain that families would soon arrive and locating their loved ones without delay or confusion was vital.

"How's it going, Duncan?"

"Oh, Phil, it's great to have you back. Dr. Barrett came through a few minutes ago and let us know that you were all right."

"Is everything going smoothly?"

"For the most part. We're at full staff, and although it looks and sounds like mass confusion, we've got things under control. I'm just verifying that our new software is doing its job—this might just be the best thing that came from the Abby audit during the disaster drill. It's looking like it's going to save us a lot of time."

"Very good, Duncan. I'm just going to make a quick walk through before I run upstairs and check in. Let me know if you need anything," Phillip said before walking down the corridor.

A new patient had just been wheeled in, and Phillip recognized him as one of the passengers on the plane. He saw Dr. Barrett in Room 4, examining the woman who was short of breath on the plane. As the surgeon looked up, he caught Phillip's eye, excused himself and walked out to talk to him.

"If it's all right, I'd like to oversee her care and run more tests to rule out a blockage. She's a little frightened right now, but she's stable. I think I'll stay with her until her daughter arrives, and then we'll discuss her options."

"I'm sure she'd appreciate that, Doctor," Phillip said as the doctor turned back into the examining room. Phillip silently observed their interactions for a minute, noting a difference in his demeanor. His gruffness seems to have softened considerably, he thought, debating silently whether it was because they had just gone through what could have been a major accident together, or if the doctor had tapped into a side of himself that he'd kept hidden for a while. Regardless of the reason, Phillip was satisfied that all was well as he made his way down the freshly waxed corridor to the "Employees Only" elevators to check in with his assistant and call Jill, knowing that she'd probably already called a dozen times to make sure he was okay.

As predicted, his assistant greeted him with, "Your wife's waiting for your call." Nodding, he grabbed a fistful of messages and walked into his office. After calling Jill and putting her mind at ease, he sat down and reflected on the past two days, knowing with all certainty that their employees would handle the day's crisis as smoothly as possible. Even Dr. Barrett.

Six Months Later...

Installing the robot had been a relatively painless process—the electricians and computer engineers had all finished their part on time and without any major glitches. Dr. Barrett had selected the first round of staff to be trained in its use, including one additional surgeon, as well as several surgical RNs and anesthesiologists. Although most of them wouldn't be responsible for the procedure, it was vital that each of them knew what to expect during the process and how it would affect their duties and responsibilities, as well as the health and medical needs of their patients.

Not only had Dr. Barrett supervised training of the robot, but he'd also been charged with educating the public about the technology. Duncan's wife, Lynne, was among the employees who had observed a change in the department chief, stating that his demeanor changed as an instructor—in that role, he exuded a great deal of patience and encouragement, which had earned him considerable respect and admiration among the staff. It was far different than their initial impression. They even noticed that he was attempting to be more courteous and patient with the staff and his patients. Maybe, just maybe, he was starting to fit in, after all.

As chief politician of the technology, Dr. Barrett had joined Phillip in hosting tours of their new wing. It was a decision that Phillip had been very comfortable making. Since their return from New York, Dr. Barrett had taken a personal interest in the image and role his department played in the hospital's reputation and community standing. He seemed to fit in with the organization more, and while being professional, was also more approachable by staff and patients alike. *Maybe he should run for political office someday, mused Phillip. He certainly has aligned his brand with that of the hospital, and I have to admit, he's been in integrity as he delivered the brand to the public. With the new surgical procedure and equipment, Barrett seemed to have taken both ownership and pride over the unit.*

Duncan had even remarked about that very fact. "You know, Phil, the day of his orientation, I predicted that someday, he'd realize that he needed the full cooperation of our employees. With the introduction of the robot, I think he now realizes that he cannot be successful by himself—he needs his staff working with him to make it happen."

Even more surprising was the fact that Dr. Barrett and Walker Briggs had formed an alliance of sorts. A mutual admiration and respect had formed between the esteemed surgeon and the personable security chief. Like most of the employees, it hadn't escaped the doctor's attention that Walker was rarely seen without this morning cup of coffee. But no one was more shocked than Walker when Dr. Barrett began routinely bringing him a cup of hot, steaming java from his favorite coffee shop, always remembering that he preferred cream and sugar. It was one of Walker's gifts, always finding that one thing in someone that he could use to open the door. With Dr. Barrett, it had been a challenge. One day, Walker had opened the door for the doctor as he briskly walked past, seemingly oblivious to anyone else. Holding a fresh cup of coffee he'd purchased from the vending machine specifically for this purpose, Walker offered it to Barrett, who replied that he wouldn't drink it. He only drank the good stuff. As he walked in the very next day, he handed a to-go cup of coffee from a well-known coffee shop and said, "Here. This is real coffee."

From that day forward, Dr. Barrett made it a regular habit, although he often accompanied his gift with, "You drink too much coffee; but if you're going to drink it anyway, don't drink the mud that comes out of those machines."

Duncan was the last to jump on board, though, and proclaim his admiration for Dr. Barrett. From day one, Barrett had rubbed him wrong with his refusal to buy into the BrandSlaughter concept. Phillip knew that the surgeon had made great strides in that area, but it wasn't until the robot had been installed and was fully operational that Duncan witnessed just how far he'd come. As was protocol whenever a new policy or procedure was implemented or offered, Phillip asked that it be taken through a trial run, and that an Audit of Brand Integrity be conducted during that run. Due to the intricacies and sophisticated computer technology involved with the procedure, though, Duncan didn't feel he was armed with enough knowledge to sufficiently audit the robot, the staff, or the procedure. So, Phillip asked Dr. Barrett to work with Duncan and assist in the audit. The results were better than any of them expected. The audit revealed only a few minor areas that needed improvement, but one of its greatest accomplishments was in giving Dr. Barrett firsthand experience in learning just how effective the audit was. Because it covered so many areas, like efficiency and productivity, accuracy, quality, and overall effectiveness, Dr. Barrett was able to get a very broad overview of how the technology would impact the hospital and its brand. In the end, he was proud of his ability to be objective and was also impressed that they had discovered a couple areas where small, but significant, improvements could be made. Not only did he recommend those improvements be made immediately, but he didn't waste any time calling his peers in New York to share the suggestions with them, as well.

When all was said and done, it was Dr. Barrett who offered Duncan an olive branch. "Duncan, there have been a lot of changes to our department since I came on board. I'd be interested in learning how we're doing— that is, if you think you and Abby have time in the next week or two."

All these events brought them to tonight's unveiling. The Board, along with a carefully selected mix of media, community leaders, and medical professionals, had been invited to the dinner and reception to celebrate the fact that Reliance Hospital was the first in the Midwest to offer minimally-invasive cardiovascular surgery. A black-tie event, it was being held in the auditorium, which had been transformed into an elegant dining hall. White linens decked the tables, and crystal water goblets sparkled across the room. The five- course dinner was being fully catered, but Phillip had vetoed their dessert choices, opting instead to provide their elite guests with a buffet of pies from nowhere else but Blues Café.

Arriving early, Duncan and Lynne met Phillip and Jill in the auditorium, marveling at its splendor. The caterers quietly came in and out, tending to last-minute details and lighting flames under hors d'oeuvres strategically located across the room. While they were taking in the delicacies, Dr. Barrett approached them and was met with good-natured laughter when he commented, "Well, it ain't Bubba's ribs, but it will do."

Before long, the room was packed. After doing the meet and greet, Phillip, Duncan, and their wives took their spot at the head table alongside   Dr. Barrett and his guest, a smart and impressive pediatrician on their staff. Dinner was first on the night's agenda, followed by a welcome address from the Chairman of the Board of Directors. Phillip was next in line, slated to introduce Dr. Barrett and the hospital's new equipment and technology. The guest speaker and star of the evening was Dr. Alexander Barrett, who would convey the amenities of the procedure to the audience and provide them with a tour of the new wing which housed the robot.

Phillip rose amidst applause after the Chairman of the Board introduced him. He approached the podium and began his speech.

"I'd like to thank each of you for participating in tonight's festivities. As most of you know, Reliance Hospital has always been committed to providing our patients with the newest medical technologies and the highest in quality care and comfort. Tonight, we will take a major step in that direction by introducing a groundbreaking medical procedure that can significantly reduce risks and recovery times for those who undergo cardiovascular surgery. Before we do, though, I'd like to take a moment to thank those who made it possible. Please give a hand to our dedicated and loyal Board of

Directors," he said, nodding toward the two tables where the Board sat with their wives and guests.

"I'd also like to thank Duncan Edwards, our brand and Chief Compliance Auditor, who has played a great role in every stage of Reliance's growth and improvement during the last ten years. Please stand, Duncan," requested Phillip, as he joined in the applause to pay respect to his friend and respected associate.

"Now, last but not least, I'd like to introduce one of the newest members of our staff. Dr. Alexander Barrett joined Reliance last year as our new cardiac surgeon and Chief of Cardiology. He is also an esteemed expert in minimally-invasive surgery and has been instrumental not only in bringing the technology and his expertise to our hospital, but also has taken the role of spokesperson in educating the community and our staff in its use. Please join me in welcoming our guest speaker, Dr. Alexander Barrett."

As the audience applauded, Phillip looked toward their table, ready to shake hands with Dr. Barrett and turn the mike over to him. But Dr. Barrett wasn't there. The applause died down as Phillip walked to the table and whispered to Duncan. "Where's Barrett?"

"Phillip, you're going to have to wing this one on your own. Dr. Barrett was just summoned to the emergency room. It's Walker. They think he's having a heart attack."

Taking Care of Your Own

After commissioning one of their other cardiologists to take over and provide a tour of the facilities, Phillip and Duncan quietly exited the auditorium, rushing to the emergency room. It wasn't difficult to determine where Walker was because virtually all of the ER staff was gathered outside his door. A quick knock on the door's frame got Dr. Barrett's attention. "May we come in?"

"Sure," nodded Barrett.

"How are you doing, Walker? Is there anything we can do?" Phillip offered.

"I'm all right. Just a scare, I guess. Don't worry about me—I'll be fine. This old heart has more miles left on it than Duncan's truck," he laughed, although his shaky voice and pale complexion failed to convince any of them.

"I'm going to hold you to that, Walker," Duncan said.

"Now, you two go back to your celebration. I'll be fine. I'll be right back here tomorrow morning, ready to go."

"We're going to head back, but only so we can finish up and then we'll be right back to check on you," Phillip said. "Dr., take good care of him, will you?"

"You bet. I'll have him doing cartwheels before you know it," said Dr. Barrett, looking up from the EKG monitor with a look of concern on his face. "But Walker's not going to be coming back tomorrow because he's not going home tonight—there is a nice bed ready for him in my department. I'm sure we can make him very comfortable."

Subdued, Phillip and Duncan returned to the auditorium where their wives were waiting. After bringing them up to speed on Walker's condition, they joined the tour group, quietly observing from the back of the room. While the cardiologist filling in for Dr. Barrett wasn't as experienced in the robot, he was representing Reliance and the technology very well. Phillip made a mental note to thank him for his contribution to the evening's success.

After the tour, the evening quickly wound to an end. The five members from the head table gathered their belongings and made their way to the cardiac unit. Dr. Barrett was in discussion with the unit's supervising RN when they approached the nurses' station.

"Hello," Dr. Barrett said, addressing them. "I'm sorry if I left you in a bind back there, but it comes with the territory."

"How's he doing?" asked Duncan, the concern evident on his face.

"He's stable and resting, which is something that's important right now. I'm still waiting for the lab results to determine if he did in fact have a heart attack, but regardless, Walker is where he needs to be for the moment. We'll be monitoring him closely and performing more tests and will be able to tell you more when we get the results."

"Is he going to be all right for the night?" asked Phillip, thinking that maybe he should also stick around, just in case Walker needed anything. They were a family at Reliance. Walker had taken care of Phillip for years—now it was Phillip's turn to return the favor.

"He is in no immediate danger," replied Dr. Barrett. "You can go home—don't worry about Walker; I'm sticking around to make sure he's all right."

Touched, Phillip thanked him. "That makes me feel better, Doctor. Thank you."

The next morning, Walker's absence from his usual spot at the hospital entrance was sorely evident. Instead of going to his office, Phillip went straight to the third floor to check on him.

Duncan had beat him there and was listening to Walker jokingly complain.

"I tell ya, Duncan, you got to get in here with Abby. The nurses don't let you sleep a wink, the coffee tastes terrible, and they won't feed me."

"You know, Alex already asked me to do that. It sounds like I better get moving on it," Duncan laughed.

"Are they not treating you well, Walker?" Phillip asked, relieved to hear that Walker's voice was stronger and his sense of humor was still intact.

"We're treating him like a king," Dr. Barrett interjected as he walked into the room, chart in hand. "On a more serious note, though, Walker, it looks like you're going to have to learn to like the coffee— it's decaf and right now, that's doctor's orders."

"All right, all right. So, what's going on, doc? You got my test results back yet? Can I go home?"

"Well, Walker, I do have some answers for you. If you don't mind, though, I'll wait until your guests to leave to share them with you."

"That's all right," Walker said, suddenly serious. "They can stay.

Go ahead, give me the news."

"Well, it appears that you do have blockages which are restricting the blood from getting to your heart. We started you on blood thinners last night, and we'll continue with that treatment. But Walker, this condition is not going away on its own. While you did not have a full-fledged heart attack, you did have a warning, and it's one that should not be ignored. To put it bluntly, Walker, you need surgery and the sooner, the better. The good news, though, is that you are a prime candidate for minimally invasive surgery using our new robot. I'd like to sit down and discuss the procedure with you and your family."

Reassurance

While Walker's son and daughter-in-law were en route from Cedar Rapids, Dr. Barrett gave an order that Walker's visitors be kept to a minimum. While everyone in the hospital wanted to stop by and wish him well, they would have to go through Dr. Barrett first, and that wouldn't be an easy feat. Phillip and Duncan were only allowed limited visits throughout the day.

When his family arrived, the receptionist requested that Security escort them to the cardiac intensive care unit, then buzzed the nursing station to let them know they were on the way.

Dr. Barrett joined the trio shortly thereafter. After a brief introduction, he got down to business. "Your father is lucky. He received a warning and hasn't suffered any damage to the heart muscle. That's a very good thing. However, our tests conclude that he is in need of a coronary bypass and possible mitral valve repair. There are two ways this can be done. Walker can undergo traditional bypass surgery, where we'll make a 12-inch incision and access his heart by splitting his breast bone and going in through the rib cage. Or, as I explained to him earlier, he can opt to undergo a relatively new procedure which uses a robot, allowing for much smaller incisions and easier access to his heart. The surgeon directs the robot's movements through a computer, which carries them out on the patient."

"What are the risks?" asked Walker's son.

"There are risks to any surgery. There are advantages and disadvantages to each, as well. Some patients aren't candidates for minimally-invasive surgery because of their health or their history. Then again, any time you perform surgery, there is a risk of infection," Barrett explained.

After spending some time answering questions, Dr. Barrett asked if they wanted time to talk before making a firm decision.

"I don't know if I'm comfortable with surgery performed by a robot. It seems too new."

"It is a newer procedure, but it has been used successfully in many cases. I've personally performed the surgery many times. The advantages include speedier recovery, less pain after surgery, less blood loss, and less opportunity for human error, such as hand tremors."

Before they went any further, Walker interjected. "I've already made my decision. Dr. Barrett has spent an extensive amount of time with me, versing me on the pros and cons. I elect the robotic surgery and have already expressed my wishes that Dr. Barrett be my surgeon."

After discussing the details and what to expect during the surgery, Dr. Barrett left to schedule Walker's surgery for the next morning, reminding them first that Walker needed his rest.

As often happens during hospitalizations, Walker's son and daughter-in-law grew familiar with the hospital in a relatively short period of time. They were soon on a first name basis with his nurses and found their way to the cafeteria several times throughout the day. Although

Walker had worked at the hospital for many years, they had never visited the facility before. During this first visit, they were impressed with what they saw.

The décor was subtle and tasteful, even in the patient rooms. Staff quietly went about their duties, mopping floors, taking vitals, making deliveries and checking on patients. Everyone they encountered was helpful and friendly, smiling and saying hello as they passed in the hallways or stopping and asking if they needed directions or assistance. All in all, they were impressed with the level of care given to both them and Walker. Although they weren't happy with the circumstances that brought them to Reliance Hospital, they felt confident that it was the right place for them to be.

Ten Weeks Later

Dr. Barrett juggled his bag and tried not to spill the hot coffee as he scampered toward the entrance.

"God only knows why you like this stuff," he said, handing over the cup. "But, at least I know it's decaf."

"The God only knows factor is the best reason to stay loyal to a brand," Walker joked. "It's like the old slogan, 'I'd rather fight than switch.'"

"That's a cigarette commercial, Walker. Don't start another bad habit that I have to cure," retorted the doctor before reaching for the door.

"Oh, by the way, happy birthday, Walker, and welcome back," he turned back with a smile.

"Thank you, Doc. I mean that. *Thank you*," Walker said, the appreciation evident in his eyes and his voice.

"Anytime, my friend," Barrett smiled.

A few minutes later, Phillip approached the entrance, right on time, Walker noted with a glance at his watch. His face lit up and he smiled as he greeted his boss. "Good morning, Mr. Dobbins. Beautiful day, isn't it?"

"Yes, Walker, it certainly is. Seeing you here this morning only makes it better."

"Thank you, sir. It's great to be here," Walker acknowledged. "Eight weeks is a long time to be away."

"Have a good day, Walker. Oh, and happy birthday," Phillip said, tucking the boxed pie under his arm that they'd share at lunch.

"I plan on doing just that, Mr. Dobbins."

Thirty minutes later, Duncan watched as Walker greeted several people entering the hospital. He was the picture of good health and happiness. His surgery had gone remarkably well and his recovery was even better than expected due to some of his new lifestyle habits with healthier food and a bit of exercise. Since then, he'd lost 20 pounds and had toned up some of the areas that age had neglected.

As he approached, Walker flashed a sincere and warm smile as he greeted the incomers. "Welcome to Reliance Hospital—please enjoy your visit."

Ahhh, Duncan thought. This is what it's all about. Walker's the perfect picture of brand integrity. Who could be better to represent our brand to the public than a satisfied customer and a satisfied employee all in one?

"For your birthday, Walker, I'm going to do you a favor," reported Duncan, as he drew near.

"What's that? Are you finally getting rid of that old clunker in the parking lot so I don't have to look at it anymore?" he teased.

"No way! That truck and I aren't parting ways—as they say, if it's not broke, don't fix it. I was referring to that fact that Me and Abby are going to audit the cafeteria today. Maybe we can help them figure out how to make coffee that meets Walker Briggs' high standards, whatever they are."

"God only knows, Duncan, because I sure don't. I just know what makes me happy."

That happiness showed as Walker turned to greet and hold the door open for a young mother holding a baby.

Walker's a gift, Duncan thought. He's proof that brand integrity starts even before a customer enters the doors. If we had lost him and his contribution to our hospital and our brand, it would have been an act of extreme BrandSlaughter.

"Happy birthday, Walker," he said. "And thank you." "For what, Duncan?" Walker asked, a little confused.

"For validating that a happy employee and a healthy patient can do amazing things for our hospital and our brand. Walker, you're more than an employee—you are everything we stand for and care about. I guess I could say you're a perfect fit, just like my truck. You're proof that when we take care of our brand, our brand takes care of us. Thanks for reminding me that failure to do just that would most certainly be an act of BrandSlaughter in the highest degree."

About the Author

DAVID M. CORBIN, Keynote Speaker and Mentor to Mentors, has been referred to as "Robin Williams with an MBA" because of his very practical, high-content speeches, coupled with entertaining and sometimes side-splitting stories and applications. A former psychotherapist with a background in healthcare, he has served as a management and leadership consultant to businesses and organizations of all sizes—from Fortune 20 companies to businesses with less than 1 million—and enjoys the challenges of all. He has worked directly with the president's office of companies such as AT&T, Hallmark, Sprint, as well as the Hon. Secretary of Veterans Administration and others. David was the host and star of the movie "Pass It On!" with his colleagues, Mark Victor Hansen, Brian Tracy, John Assaraf, Denis Waitley, Greg Reid, Evander Holyfield, Les Brown and 50 others. David is featured in the Napoleon Hill Foundation's movie, Three Feet From Gold and the book of the same name which became the#3 best-selling book in America.

David's book, Illuminate-Harnessing the Positive Power of Negative Thinking (John Wiley & Sons Publishing) has reached the #1 bestselling book Amazon category of business life. He has been a featured speaker for INC Magazine's national and regional business conferences since 1995 and was rated in their top 5% of speakers. His full-service consulting and development firm specializes in maximizing the productivity and profitability of business, industry, and government.

David was awarded the International Enterprise of the Year for Innovation by Bank of America for the touch screen patient interview system that he co-invented and took to market. Presented by Former Prime Minister Margaret Thatcher, Sec. James Baker, Tom Peters, Maya Angelou, Hon. Newt Gingrich and others.

Preventing Brandslaughter

David M. Corbin
Best Selling Author, Keynote Speaker,
Business Adviser, Inventor, Producer

Contact for David's Keynotes and MacroMentoring
Program.

Email: Melanie@DavidCorbin.com

Email: david@davidcorbin.com

Phone: +1 858 748 6060

explore the following website:
http://davidcorbin.com

Made in the USA
San Bernardino, CA
10 February 2018